PRAISE FOR AT·ONE·MENT

Thomas McConkie is a fellow traveler, walking some paths I know and others I do not. This book is born of struggle and of grace, but there's nothing stodgy about the wisdom you'll find on offer in these pages: it is warm, welcoming, and humorous. Thomas's simple, beautiful prose invites readers to take the first, or the next, step on their own paths of self-knowledge and self-transformation, with hearts set ablaze for "at-one-ment."
—CHARLES STANG, director of the Center for the Study of World Religions, Harvard Divinity School

I loved this beautifully written book! McConkie teaches us rich spiritual concepts in an elegant and accessible way. He offers a rich, personal understanding of the relationship of faith, sin, repentance, and embodiment to the divinity within and around us. He gives us a glimpse of what spiritual aliveness is and what it offers our souls in the struggle of everyday mortality. I haven't read a better articulation of what we are reaching towards in a fallen world than this.
—JENNIFER FINLAYSON-FIFE, sex and relationship educator and therapist

If a primary purpose of the Restoration is to "gather together in one all things in Christ" (Ephesians 1:10), then Thomas McConkie is one of the more profound practitioners of this outward-looking, inward-embracing work. Drawing upon his deep knowledge of spiritual development and his rich experience in meditative practice, he invites contemplation into the process of the ongoing Restoration, gently guiding readers into principles and practices that powerfully illustrate what it means to "be still and know that I am God" (Psalm 46:10). To anyone looking to build their faith, calm their mind, and reach at-one-ment at deeper, more soul-expanding levels, please read this book.
—JARED HALVERSON, associate professor of ancient scripture, Brigham Young University, host of *Unshaken*

AT ONE MENT

Embodying the Fullness
of Human-Divinity

THOMAS WIRTHLIN MCCONKIE

FaithMatters

FAITH MATTERS

Copyright © 2023 by Thomas Wirthlin McConkie
All rights reserved.

No part of this publication may be reproduced or used in any manner without the prior written permission of the publisher, except for the use of brief quotations in critical reviews.

To request permissions, contact the publisher at info@faithmatters.org.

Paperback: 978-1-953677-16-7
Ebook: 978-1-953677-18-1
Audiobook: 978-1-953677-17-4

Library of Congress Number: 2023946724

Printed in the United States of America

Faith Matters Publishing
2929 W Navigator Drive, Suite 400
Meridian, ID 83642

faithmatters.org

*To Dan and Lis,
for planting gospel seeds in my
heart from the very beginning.*

Contents

ACKNOWLEDGMENTS	xv
A NOTE BEFORE WE BEGIN	xvii
PREFACE	xix

CHAPTER 1
The Human-Divine — 1

An Ordinary Moment	1
Guiding Principles for the Road Ahead	7
1. Your Direct Experience Is the Only Teacher	8
2. Don't Be Afraid to Get a Little Messy	9
3. Being Clear on What You Value Will Give You Direction	11
4. You Are Already Whole	13
A Look Ahead	17

CHAPTER 2
Increase in Being — 21

The Body's Knowing	26
Body Loathing	28
Entering into God's Rest (Meditation)	30
Fulfillment of Our Divine Being	30
The Heart's Knowing	33
The Mind's Knowing	38
Pitfalls of the Thinking Mind	40
Embodied at All Levels	42
Embodying Fullness (Meditation)	46

FIRST INTERLUDE
Investigating the Self — 47

CHAPTER 3
An Eye Single — 51

High States of Concentration — 51
A Brief History of Concentration Practices — 52
Filled with Light — 57
The Role of Practice — 61
Worship — 63
Life Practice: Consecrating Your Attention — 66
Concentration as Trust — 67
Unifying the Mind — 69
Fall Behind the Display — 73
Resting in Stillness — 76
Introduction to Remembrance — 78
Remembrance (Meditation) — 78
Light Knows the Mind — 78
Introduction to Open-Focus — 80
Open-Focus (Meditation) — 80

CHAPTER 4
The Sacred Heart — 81

The Dancing Walls of the Chapel — 81
Did Not Our Hearts Burn within Us? — 84
The Subtle Heart — 85
Embracing Joy *and* Sorrow — 87
Noise and Signal — 91
The Heart and Mind in Concert — 94
Radical Repentance — 99
Some of My Favorite Heart-Openers — 103

Heart Practice: Asking a Real Question (Meditation)	104
Lectio Divina (Introduction)	105
Read, Ponder, Pray, Rest (Meditation)	105
A Heart of Flesh	106
Knowing from the Heart (Meditation)	108
Heart Yoga	108
Heart Yoga (Meditation)	109
Come What May and Love It	109
Come What May and Love It (Meditation)	110

CHAPTER 5
Divine Vulnerability — 111

The Developing Self	113
Core Vulnerabilities	115
Energy Centers	118
Sin	121
Energy Centers in Scripture	123
Our New Nature in Christ	126
Examples of the Energy Centers from Everyday Life	128
Safety	129
Pleasure	130
Esteem	131
Power	132
Right Relationship with the Energy Centers	133
Exploring Your Own Energy Centers (Meditation)	135
Healing across the Generations	136
On Obedience and Divine Vulnerability	139
Practicing Unconditional Kindness (Meditation)	142

SECOND INTERLUDE
The Infinite Self — 143

DIAGRAM
Creation, Fall, Atonement 148

CHAPTER 6
Transformations of Faith **151**

God's Orchestra 151
A Brief History 154
A Simple Developmental Map 155
Zero-Person Perspective 157
First-Person Perspective 158
    Gifts of the First-Person Perspective 159
Second-Person Perspective 162
    Gifts of the Second-Person Perspective 162
    Pitfalls of the Second-Person Perspective 164
    Holy Envy 165
Third-Person Perspective 167
    Gifts of the Third-Person Perspective 168
        Technologies 168
        Self as Object of Investigation 169
        From Commandment to Commitment 170
    Pitfalls of Third-Person Perspective 172
    Perfect and Progressing (Meditation) 175
The Rhythm of Development 175
Diagram: Person Perspectives 177
Fourth-Person Perspective 182
    Gifts of the Fourth-Person Perspective 182
    Pitfalls of the Fourth-Person Perspective 186
Fifth-Person Perspective 190
    Gifts of the Fifth-Person Perspective 192
    Pitfalls of the Fifth-Person Perspective 193
From Fifth- to Sixth-Person Perspective 195

The Harvest	198
Infinite Life in Christ (Meditation)	199

CHAPTER 7
At-One-Ment **201**

A Look Back at Some Key Landmarks	203
Expect Dramatic Results	205
Yesterday's Tonic Is Today's Toxin	208
Just Messing Around with the Ego	211
Living Stones	215
Life, Love, and Light (Meditation)	217
Uniquely Personal, Universally Divine	217

ENDNOTES **222**

Acknowledgments

I REMEMBER a frosty morning in February 2020 sitting with Bill and Susan Turnbull in downtown Salt Lake—on their anniversary, in fact. They invited me to articulate what I had learned about human development and transformation in my career. The initial fruits of that conversation were an online course offered at Faith Matters called "Transformations of Faith." A few months after the release, Bill called me up and commented that the transcripts of the course read a lot like a book. I liked the idea of spending more time with the impromptu language of the course and crafting it into something more systematic and precise. Neither the online course nor this book would exist without the Turnbulls' original vision. This project has been a profound blessing for me to work on.

Numerous editors and writers more talented than myself have steered me along the way. Special thanks go to Jon Ogden, who in addition to being an insightful editor is doing work I greatly admire at Uplift Kids, helping families explore expansive spirituality. He is a beautiful embodiment of the path I hope to lay out in this book. I'm also indebted to Rachael Givens Johnson, Austin Andrus, and, yes, Bill Turnbull for their insights and editorial prowess. My wife, Gloria Pak, remains my muse and personal wisdom teacher. She is subtle beyond words and has spent countless hours with me going on long walks, trawling through inspired texts, and engaging me in spirited debate, all in service of helping me give more beautiful shape to these teachings.

Finally, I offer a deep bow of gratitude to John Kesler. It has been his mentorship and influence on me over many years now that have slowly opened me to the majesty of the restored gospel in its current form and all that has yet to be revealed.

A Note Before We Begin

THROUGHOUT THIS BOOK you will see an unconventional use of capital letters. I capitalize certain words (e.g., *Light, Manifestation*) to invoke a sense of the Divine, even to call on names of the Divine that we're not used to recognizing as such. Traditionally in Christianity and the restored gospel, we capitalize a rather restricted set of names that refer to God: Jehovah, Heavenly Father and Mother, Christ, and so forth. My preference is to broaden this convention. In Islam, it is customary to speak of the ninety-nine names of Allah. Surely there are even more names for the Divine than that.

Also, according to Latter-day Saint theology, God is comprised of Heavenly Parents—Father and Mother—who were once human as we are. They live in this universe in the same way that we do; They did not create it. By learning to obey and embody what we might call Cosmic Law, They progressed in their divine stature to a point where They could organize us, Their spirit children, in such a way that allows us to progress in our divinity alongside Them in covenantal relationships.

Therefore, when I use the term God in this book, I am referring to Heavenly Parents.

When I wish to point to the Reality that gestates and organizes the universe, that exalts nature and makes divinity possible, I will use terms such as *Sacred, Divine Reality, Holiness*, and so forth. Most religious traditions simply refer to this foundational reality as "God."

Finally, you will see me use the words *atonement* and *atone* differently than you may have seen them used before. I believe the restored gospel offers a much more expansive way to understand and experience Christ's project of "at-one-ment." In addition to treating the Atonement as a historic event, I invite the reader to explore the developmental and contemplative dimensions of atonement that are always present and available to us right now. As evolving beings of Intelligence and Light, we can at-one with more and more of Sacred Reality, generating new Worlds in this Infinitely Divine process.

Preface

FOR THE LAST TWENTY-FIVE YEARS of my life, I've had a practice. Some would call it an obsession. It began with a need in my late teens to be healed. I felt so much pain inside back then that I would have done anything to escape myself. Somewhere along the way, my fundamental sense of *self* shifted. It happened so gradually I didn't even know it was happening. This new life snuck up on me.

I no longer felt like the one who had been shattered into a thousand shards and slivers of glass. Somehow I had become the one who was aware of the brokenness. Though what had felt like "me" still felt obliterated at times, from my new identity as awareness—to my surprise—I felt quite light, quite free. So free, in fact, I found I could inhabit the pain from a new place entirely—one of radical love.

This book is about that path of waking up to new, divine realities—Life, Love, and Light. It's about letting go of who we believed we were and becoming who we actually are. I call this "practice."

To become who we actually are, it turns out, is strangely difficult. Experience has taught me that we are all quite expert at defending against the intense vulnerability that being our true self implies. The author Bruno Barnhart put it well when he said, "We humans prefer a manageable complexity to an unmanageable simplicity." Well, we may *prefer* the "manageable complexity," but our hearts *yearn* for the simplicity. Our souls cry out for this redemption.

Which brings me to another key element of this book. I was raised Latter-day Saint in a good family that loves the gospel. From early childhood, I loved learning about Jesus but didn't always love religion—a dichotomy I won't attempt to unpack at the moment. In my adolescence and twenties, I drifted far from the faith tradition that formed me in my early years. And then all at once, in that moment where my basic sense of identity shifted, Christ set my heart ablaze.

Some would call this a conversion experience, and truthfully, I'm quite comfortable with that. I remember the instant my heart was converted to Christ for eternity. There are no words for that *Holiness*. The more His Divine Influence works in my life, transforming me through Spirit and Grace, the more mysterious it all is to me.

I am also aware that the name *Christ* can mean very different things to different people. Some have used that name to justify all manner of violence. Others have called Christ their inspiration for performing acts of loving service that seem to go beyond mere human capacity. When I use the name *Christ*, I'm referring to what feels in my body and heart like a *Gravity* that has been attracting me since before my parents were born. This Gravity feels to me like Love itself—with absolutely no discernible beginning or end. Not only is it a cosmic force at play, but it is also at once achingly personal and intimate. Through Christ I feel that I am *felt* and know that I am *known*.

While I learned to recognize this Immense Love as "Christ" in my native language and faith tradition, I cannot doubt that this same Gravity is raising up all of creation even now to its own Sacred sphere.

I see Christ everywhere and in everyone. My Buddhist brothers and sisters see me and all sentient beings as sharing what they call Buddha Nature. For many in the Hindu world, Lord Krishna ignites them with Divine Love and calls their souls to transcendence. And still, there are the indigenous traditions, too numerous to name, each of them sacred to the core and animated by a Spirit that reveals to us we are all kin.

I want to express this at the outset because I recognize that the transformative path is utterly unique to each of us. Being a limited person with relatively narrow perspectives and experience, I can only point to the Mystery with the language and symbols that are familiar to me. And I know from painful personal experience that in calling *Sacred Reality* one name and not another, some will read my words and feel dealt out of the conversation. That is not my heart's intent.

In what follows, I'll use the language that feels most appropriate to me, trusting that you too will use the language that is most appropriate for you. No matter the names we give the moon and the tides, the moon's gravity causes the ocean to swell and to heave all the same. So it is with Christ, with the Gravity that draws me towards the eternities with you, the reader, whoever you are and whatever wild songs resound in your heart of hearts.

AT·ONE·MENT

Chapter 1

The Human-Divine

AN ORDINARY MOMENT

The territory I will attempt to describe to you in the coming pages is Holiness itself. To me, it is no less than the pearl of great price—worth trading everything you have for it once you find it. And the truly good news? It's not off in some distant land. It's the very Ground that supports you right now.

    I have a story about how I was initiated on this path. It's an ordinary story, but I think you'll find as you read on in this book that it's the ordinary moments that are in fact extraordinary. When I was thirteen years old, I suddenly, and somewhat inexplicably, decided that I didn't want to go to church anymore. My parents, devout Latter-day Saints, were consternated and ultimately unwilling to "go gentle into that good night." We clashed bitterly over my rebellion throughout my high school years. My fallen status in the family seemed to cast a shadow over everything. I came of age in that shadow, that dank, moldy environment where hurt feelings festered and resentments multiplied like spores.

How can I describe that time to you? I was a walking oxymoron: a functionally non-Mormon McConkie, gentile heir of General Authority blood. It was as if my life was forfeit because I'd failed to do the one thing that everybody from my family was expected to do: be a stalwart Latter-day Saint. I had gone and failed so early and so fully at the one thing that mattered, failing beyond that seemed inconsequential. At that point, my life became a race to the bottom—a cocktail of illicit and psychiatric drugs, copious drinking, and heroic levels of truancy. It is an indictment on the school system that they allowed me to graduate.

Freshly stamped out by the conveyor belt of public education, I prepared to do exactly nothing after high school. During that extended dark night, I had no star to orient myself to. Every direction felt as unpromising as the next, so naturally I stood still. My mom pleaded with me to apply to the local college so that my life didn't stall entirely. Not having a plan B, or plan A for that matter, I signed the application she'd filled out for me. My inauspicious career in higher education thus began in spite of myself.

When fall came around, I moved out of my parents' house and into my first-ever apartment. After unpacking a few boxes and throwing some sheets over a spartan twin mattress, I realized, with anguish, that my whole life seemed to be hanging together by a thread.

Lying awake in bed each night was a silent beating. Corrosive thoughts of everything I'd failed to become burned in my brain like battery acid. Somehow in the fog of my melancholy, an idea that didn't seem to be my own appeared to me: "I should learn to meditate." I didn't even know what meditation was. I didn't even know that I knew the word *meditation* until it wafted through my bedroom window one sleepless night. Later, in true Zen form, I came to think of that impression as an answer to a prayer I'd never said.

"How am I going to learn to meditate?" I asked myself. "What does it even *mean* to meditate?" Mind you, this all took place long before you could get on a search engine and look up your local mindfulness center. This was the late '90s. I still didn't have my first email address, and meditation for most people where I'm from evoked images of gaunt yogis and pagan devilry.

I started asking around, nevertheless. I was bussing tables at a swanky seafood restaurant in downtown Salt Lake at the time and surveyed my coworkers. "Do you know anything about meditation?" I'd ask a bit sheepishly. It turned out that a few people did know a little something about it. Before long, I was attending my first daylong meditation retreat with a Zen master who lived right in my neighborhood. The game was afoot.

Gracefully, I was in a state of complete desperation. I say *gracefully* because one particular form of Grace I've come to appreciate in life is when nothing else is working, we have no other choice. The only way out for me was *through*. If meditation didn't work, I didn't know what else I would do. I'd already seen a psychiatrist for years and was amply medicated. I was exercising and trying to eat healthy. But I needed medicine that went soul-deep.

Channeling all the unexploited religious zeal of my youth, I began sitting myself down every single evening to practice meditation. I can't remember how long each session was at first, maybe thirty minutes or so. But I remember it being mildly terrifying every time I confronted myself in the silence. Secrets I'd carefully kept from myself for years through busyness and distraction percolated to the surface and revealed their demonic form.

Taming the physical body was also a big problem when I got started. After a few minutes of settling in awkwardly to a seated position on the floor, the stabbing pain in my back mocked me, as if to say, "What is it that you think you're trying to accomplish here?" My mind wandered like a stray dog rooting around for scraps from dumpster to dumpster. Still, I kept practicing.

Around six months later, I was walking home from campus. My apartment was just a couple blocks away from President's Circle at the University of Utah. The walk home was downhill, due east, overlooking the Salt Lake Valley. I remember sauntering down the hill, pleasantly relaxed, when out of nowhere, a gentle, full-body sensation bloomed in my awareness. I noted my breath had already shifted, dropping down from the shallow chest breathing typical of low-grade anxiety to a more cavernous breath, reaching into the dark, silky recesses of my abdomen. I realized all at once that my breathing had been changing over the last several months of meditation practice, and just now, in this moment, the breath was doing its meditation thing all on its own. I was being *meditated*.

I found myself almost gliding home. My belly was soft, my whole body relaxed. I had never spontaneously felt so restful all at once. The current of anxiety I'd grown so used to—like a downed electrical wire buzzing through my brain all those years—fell silent. It was as if God had reached down and shut off the power supply.

Everything was different.

Let me be clear—I'm not talking about a spiritual light rending the heavens. I didn't see Jesus walking by my side that evening, reassuring me he'd been there all along. My body simply relaxed. But that, *exactly that*, was heaven to me. It was more than I knew I could ask for. If I'd had a genie and a lamp back then and all I could wish for was to stop being so anxious and finally sleep through the night, that would have been *more than enough*.

Here I was, strolling around in a brand-new, more-than-enough world, resting deeply as I walked. Not only did I feel restful, but all the world around me felt restful too. I looked out across the valley as I felt the softness of my animal body moving about, breathing in its native simplicity. Gratitude overcame me. In a way I wasn't expecting and didn't even know was possible, I was healed.

Later that evening, somewhere in the afterglow, the thought came to me, "This is what meditation does?! This is what breathing for thirty minutes a night does?!" It was one of the most significant transformations of my entire life. And that was only a few months into the practice.

Had that been the only benefit I received from meditation practice, that single shift would have made way for a whole new life. And yet, twenty-five years later, I see that moment differently. As revelatory as it was at the time, it now feels almost trivial compared to the transformations I've experienced through practice and Grace since then.

After my "mini awakening" while coming home from campus that day, I began to understand something that has come to steer the course of my life: *by paying attention to how we pay attention, we can transform beyond what we imagined was possible.* In my case, by shifting my attention from neurotic, depressive, obsessive thoughts to my breath for a little time each day, one of the greatest spiritual breakthroughs of my life ensued. In my own small way, I was learning there are practices we can engage in that can change the very substance of our being.

I started out as a diligent meditator by necessity—if it didn't work, I was dead in the water. But that do-or-die mentality gradually shifted into a simple and genuine love for the contemplative life. I was discovering little by little what it meant to "live prayerfully." Meditation has since become one of the most important tools I use when working with others. I regard meditation as a foundational skill that supports other transformative practices. Incidentally, when I say "meditation," I mean any practice of intentionally guiding attention towards what we value most, including Buddhist still sitting, Christian contemplation, Sufi zikr, and more. For me, *meditation* represents a whole spectrum of contemplative practices that all involve *paying attention to how we're paying attention and thereby choosing what we take to be a worthy object of concentration.* What we pay attention to over time will change us in dramatic ways. What we pay attention to is ultimately what we worship.

By my late twenties, I was coming to appreciate the contemplative core of the world's wisdom traditions. It turns out that virtually all sacred traditions in their own way value high states of concentration as a portal to the transcendent. Buddhism offered me my first glimpse into this sacred world revealed through the undivided mind. But once I took the contemplative view, it became obvious to me that an eye kept single on the Glory of God in a Christian context revealed its own awesome realities. Quite by accident, through the practice of daily meditation, my eyes were opened to a new earth that Christ had set ablaze in the heart of Eternity. I could never deny that Reality again. Beyond Buddhism and Christianity, I found myself intrigued by what all the traditions uniquely had to say about transformative spiritual practice. What are the distinct approaches to transformation in the broader tradition of humanity itself? It turns out all cultures, all traditions have ideas—really good ideas—about how to improve, even perfect, the human being.

It's not just ancient wisdom where we find the idea of perfecting the human being, either. While meditation practice was my initial entry point into transformative practice, it didn't stop there. About seven years into my soul's contemplative voyage, I formed a keen interest in developmental psychology, particularly in the way that adults can continue to grow and transform throughout their lives. I began doing formal research in the field and started to facilitate cohort-based groups of adults who wanted to intentionally explore this challenging terrain with the support of a community.

Ultimately, I'm committed to understanding any ancient or modern wisdom, any insight and revelation that can help *all of us* embody the fullness of human-divinity. Personally, this study has taken me deep into Buddhism and Christianity as sacred traditions and also into modern neuroscience, developmental psychology, integral theory, and a host of other disciplines that our forebears didn't have access to. You'll experience this integration of ancient and modern, sacred and secular throughout the book. Above all, my hope is that my love for all that is sacred shines through and that it celebrates truth, "let it come from whence it may."[1]

This book is not and cannot be an exhaustive exploration. Whatever I'm able to express in the coming pages, I know there will always be more to discover. What I hope to offer is a glimpse into new realms of Divine Reality. You may find meaningful connection with all of the practices I share here, but even if you only connect with one of them, I'd encourage you to keep going with that one. A single seed brings forth a mighty harvest when cared for.

Metamorphosis, awakening, transformation—whatever words we use to describe this mysterious process—is our birthright as human beings. Something, forever Holy, seeks to realize Itself in us, through us, and *as us*. This Holiness calls for our participation and wholehearted engagement in the Life Divine. We are all searching. We must not stop until we find.

GUIDING PRINCIPLES FOR THE ROAD AHEAD

Before properly diving in, I'll highlight four guiding principles that I think will help you get the most out of this book. In addition, I've provided practice sections throughout the book to help you integrate the learning more deeply and make this process uniquely your own. I also encourage you to take time with the guided meditations throughout the book. To access these recordings, just scan the QR code next to the meditation with your smartphone camera, and tap on the link that appears.

1. Your Direct Experience Is the Only Teacher

Perhaps the most important thing I can say is that your direct experience is the only teacher. I can share my experience with you, using the most effective language I can, to point to different realities in the transformative process. But at the end of the day, you'll have to try these perspectives on for yourself, or not. If I'm doing my job well, you'll read something, *feel* something, and it will wake up what is *already inside of you*. You'll know by the way it tastes that it's good and that you can let it deeply in, that you can trust your experience.

If you read something here that tastes bad to you, by all means, *spit it out*. Or if you don't want to spit it out entirely, you can take a taste and set it down somewhere out of the way and maybe come back to it later. Some tastes are acquired, after all.

Above all, transformation is an intimate process of getting to know yourself at the deepest level. It's not about adopting what some author thinks in all his preferences, prejudices, and blind spots. The process is personal to each of us. What works for one doesn't work for another. And what works for you today may not work tomorrow. Yes, I have some experience that I believe is worth sharing. But your discerning wisdom, your knowing heart, and the feedback you get from life itself are some of the most reliable assets you have on this path.

PRACTICE

Step back from yourself and notice your basic orientation to life with respect to connecting and separating energies:

- *Do you tend to lose touch with your personal sense of authority in the face of others' opinions (connecting energy), or do you*

> tend to isolate yourself from others and do your own thing, no matter what wisdom others are sharing (separating energy)?

- *If you tend towards connecting energy, try on the possibility of anchoring in your own authority more and not cueing off of other's opinions so often.*
- *If you tend towards separating energy, try on the possibility of being more vulnerable by letting new perspectives affect you more deeply.*

2. Don't Be Afraid to Get a Little Messy

The next principle I want to highlight is that transformation is not always, but often is, a messy, halting affair. This principle can feel at odds with a culture that recounts our preeminent example of transformation—Jesus Christ—tracing a beeline from manger to God's right hand without a single misstep. The way the record comes to us in the New Testament, we have precious few details of Jesus as a youth, then a gaping hole right up to the final years of his ministry. All at once, we see Christ performing miracles and calling down the kingdom of God.

I'm not complaining—the scriptural record is what it is. I personally find it to be transcendently beautiful more often than not. But the gaps in the record present a particular challenge when we try to use it as a how-to manual. The question arises: "How do I transform through the nitty-gritty details of my life?" I mean, was Jesus a moody teenager? Did he have doubts about his vocation as a carpenter? What I've found in the Christian tradition is that sometimes we tend to bring a magical mentality to the process of development. Because we don't have the play-by-play of how Jesus developed into the stature of a god, we assume that it just kind of spontaneously happened as a foregone conclusion. We then tend to superimpose this unrealistic expectation onto our own lives. Not thinking about it too carefully, we suppose the following: "Life is really hard, but one day something is going to happen. I don't know when or how—I think it's after we die—but something big will happen and I will transform. Everything will be different then."

My experience on the path is that this kind of magical thinking is inimical to the reality of development, which must unfold line upon line in the messy details of our lives. Said another way, our relationship to time is a direct reflection of our relationship to Eternity. If we can't accept Eternity on its own terms right now, who says we're going to be able to accept it later? We run the risk of continually rejecting the *Glory of Now*, wrongly supposing that a more agreeable *now* will come later. It will not. Or if it does, what is agreeable to us then will at some point become disagreeable again, and we will never get off the merry-go-round of misery, perpetually waiting for conditions to change in our favor.

So, my invitation here is to inhabit your exalted human messiness and notice any limiting beliefs, such as "It shouldn't be this hard" or "Other people don't seem to struggle as much as I do." Or, the classic, "I must be doing it wrong." Maybe your "wrong" is exactly what you need to find your way to a deeper "right." Maybe exactly this mess is consecrated for your gain.

There is no magic wand someone will wave to translate you from a sniveling, suffering human being into an exalted *heavenly* being. This process that you and I are so intimately involved in is just that: a process.

I remember a related experience I had when I moved to Spain after graduating from college. My whole life I'd grown up in Latter-day Saint culture where people spoke of missionaries having the gift of tongues. I imagined they entered a magical womb at the Missionary Training Center and were reborn only weeks later as fluent speakers of Russian, Mandarin, or Swahili.

About two months into my stay in Spain, I was getting a better ear for the language and even starting to string some decent-sounding sentences together. All at once, an intuition that had been smoldering in my subconscious burst into a realization: "I'm learning Spanish one word at a time, one phrase at a time, one situation at a time." I realized that this process was gradual and organic—that with enough time and attention, I would master the language.

I still believe in the gift of tongues. But in that moment I understood the works side of the "grace and works" equation with respect to language learning. Lived experience replaced the magical thinking of my youth. The process of transformation is no different. There is a lot of Grace and magic involved. *And* it requires a lot of time and attention on our part, a lot of sincere intent.

As I see it, there is nothing about the process unfolding *right now* in time that is fundamentally separate from Eternity. When we let that in, when we realize that the *Now* is all we ever have to work with, we tend to relax a little bit. Hopefully we quit fantasizing about the easy life, free of disturbance, where God will eventually sort it all out for us. We start to take personal responsibility for our moment-to-moment response to life. How we respond to each moment is how we grow into the stature of eternal beings. We can learn to include disturbance, setbacks, and heartbreak in the fullness of all that is. This is it. Eternity is right *now*. When we accept this principle, we can embrace the often messy transformative process on a new level.

3. Being Clear on What You Value Will Give You Direction

The next principle I would point out is that it's helpful to become clear on what you truly value on this path. In a relative way, as human beings, there are things we value, and there are things we value less.

Take your favorite restaurant for example. You probably don't go too often because it's a bit pricey, and you like to save it for special occasions. But the food is so exquisite that you go there again and again and you're willing to spend good money. Next, think about how much you pay for fast food—a bean burrito, a greasy burger—whatever your pleasure. There are meals we pay very little for because we recognize the quality is relatively low. And there are meals we pay ten times what we'd pay somewhere else because the cuisine starts to resemble art more than food.

The spiritual journey is like this, in a way. Think about the human beings you know who embody the most sublime qualities. You know by their presence and how they treat others that there's a highly refined humanity in them. Their lives are works of art. The most natural thing in the world is to want to emulate people like this. You want to be like them, and you're willing to invest time and attention to grow in that direction.

I'm reminded of one of my wife's sublime qualities as I write. She has a way of being present in a group of people and tracking with precise detail what everyone is thinking and feeling. She can then say just the thing that needs to be said. Like a homeopathic drop in the tonic, she brings more honesty and depth to a conversation with the simplest gesture. I've seen her do this countless times. She says the thing that others didn't even realize was unspoken until she says it. Once she says it, the whole room lets out an energetic sigh and everyone can relax more in their own skin. The atmosphere in the room begins to sparkle and people marvel at her wizardry—her refined humanity.

On the other end of the spectrum, it doesn't take me long to find examples of my own clunkiness, my unrefined humanity. Recently, I got upset with my brother for trampling on our new Japanese grass that's still struggling to get established. I found myself barking at him, "Off the grass, man! How could you not see that there?" The moment I felt my irritation surge in my body and spew out my mouth, I regretted it. I knew I shouldn't talk to him like that. I could only apologize, stand back, and marvel at how rough a stone I still am.

When my wife is fully present in a group of people, releasing them into new heights of divinity, it's clear that something transformative is taking place. To extend the restaurant metaphor I started earlier, the dinner guests "ooh" and "aah" at her culinary skill. Whereas in my moments of irritation and impatience, I'm like a soggy side of day-old french fries.

I offer these examples to invite you from the outset to reflect on the human-divine qualities you genuinely admire. I recommend focusing on one or two of them at a time for as long as you feel you need: humility, childlike wonder, playfulness, forgiveness, generosity of spirit—whatever attracts you. The heightened awareness of virtuous qualities you intend to develop will bring power and focus to your practice. Don't be shy to acknowledge the less admirable qualities that show up in your behavior as well—we'll dedicate an entire chapter to those later on.

We each walk a unique path and are given spiritual gifts. Becoming clear on what we love and admire helps us be more intentional about what plants we want to grow in our garden.

REFLECTION QUESTION:

Journal on the questions below. Spend some time here. This exercise will help you make this transformative process your own:

- *What qualities do I value and admire? What qualities do I intend to cultivate at this time in my life? Who are examples that embody these qualities I wish to cultivate?*

Take some time to let these questions breathe, and feel free to elaborate on them.

4. You Are Already Whole

I mentioned Grace above. I want to say a bit more about it here because, in a sense, it is the ultimate principle of transformation. I can hardly overstate its importance. But when I say "Grace," I mean something very particular. In a theological sense, *Grace* refers to love unearned. Heavenly Parents give us Their love as an act of Divine Generosity without qualification. That's part of what I mean by Grace. But I also want to go a little deeper.

As we hold the intention to improve ourselves and transform, there's a natural tendency to feel like we're the ones doing it all. We think, "I'm the one who picked up this book and am taking the time to study it. It's me who has a desire to become a better person. *I'm* doing the work of transformation."

But after we've been on this path for a while, we become sensitive to a more subtle quality of question: "What was it in me that sought to transform in the first place? What is it in me that yearns to wake up to Divine Reality?" When these questions arise, they open up a whole new dimension of life. We begin to sense that something is happening, but "I" don't seem to be doing it. But if I'm not the one doing it, then *who* or *what* is?

Christ points to this Grace in a teaching from the Sermon on the Mount when He says, "Blessed are they which do hunger and thirst after righteousness, for they shall be filled" (Matthew 5:6, KJV).

On a subtle level, we can notice that hunger and thirst for righteousness is *itself* righteousness. What is it that cries out in us—that repents and wishes to be transformed—but righteousness itself? It is *like* seeking *like*.

One way of understanding Christ's teaching is that the hunger and thirst in each of us is already a manifestation of Divine Grace living through us. This presence of Grace means that as you engage in the process of transformation, you can relax in a way that perhaps you've never let yourself relax. It means that *right now, already, always now, you can be One with the very Love that you seek.*

We balk at this. It sounds too good to be true. The part of us that feels flawed, imperfect, lacking in too many ways to name—that *natural man or woman*—will gladly engage in self-improvement projects till the end of time. After all, as long as we're seeking self-improvement, we have the perfect excuse to not accept ourselves exactly as we are and therefore to not accept God exactly as God is.

But there is another dimension to Sacred Reality. Beyond time, beyond doing or not doing, in this moment, right now, your essence and God's essence are One. There is no separation. You hunger and thirst after righteousness because your essence is *already* righteousness. You are being drawn to the Wholeness that is already here.

As we realize this truth—that we are always already grounded in Divine Wholeness—the yoke becomes easy, the burden light. You can laugh when you catch yourself making the same old mistakes, when you get frustrated at the same things you promised you wouldn't get frustrated with. Paradoxically, when we connect to our inherent Divine Wholeness, we become better, not worse, at self-improvement. Knowing we're good to the core, transformation takes on a quality of play. No longer consumed by a chronic sense of deficit and lack, we realize: "I don't *need* to change in order to be lovable, so why not try something new?" In a sense, the stakes couldn't be lower!

The point is, by connecting to Wholeness first, Wholeness itself will motivate us, not fear and lack. You don't have to *hate yourself forward* anymore. You don't have to read this book on spirituality because you're not spiritual enough. You do the things you do as a celebration of who you already are in your essence. And if you become something new along the way—well, that will be good too.

When I share this dimension of the path with others, there is a particular fear that comes up. People are afraid if they open up to this radical Grace they'll become lazy and complacent. "If I take myself to be 'whole,' will I even want to get out of bed? Why do anything at all if I'm already perfect?" The question itself betrays how accustomed we are to motivating ourselves from a place of perfectionism and striving. We strive in order to compensate for our sense of lack. This mentality inevitably leads to burnout: the more we strive, the more our striving confirms to us that we need to strive even more.

However, the more we learn to rest in Divine Wholeness—our own inherent Wholeness—the more we draw on Infinite Energy to go about doing good. Not because we have to. But because it is our nature to do so. Suzuki Roshi captured this "both-and" reality humorously when he said to his students, "Each of you is perfect the way you are… and you can use a little improvement."[2] When we touch our inherent Perfection, we naturally seek to improve. Only, everything is different now: the burnout energy of perfectionism gives way to the delicious flavor of effortless accomplishment.

Admittedly, this dimension of ourselves is different enough from what we've been taught by the world that it can take a little while to start to trust. Don't take my word for it, of course, but try living with this possibility for a little while and see what happens. Imagine: What if who you are *right now* isn't a deficit to be compensated for but a Wholeness that desires to express itself uniquely through you? What if even your distrust of the possibility that you are *Whole* is a feature of your Wholeness?

When we connect to this dimension of our human-divinity, we no longer seek in order to escape a sense of deficit or lack. Rather, we start from Fullness and spill over into greater Fullness. We are agents of the Divine Life, and we know it. Our cup is always running over.

PRACTICE:

Find a place where you can sit comfortably and undisturbed for a length of time. After settling in, notice any sense of busyness coming up—a feeling like you just don't have time to sit around and "do nothing." Let that wave of sensation pass again and again. Learn to see what's on the other side of that familiar feeling of busyness.

Next, notice any thoughts coming up, especially judgmental thoughts and limiting beliefs you hold about yourself. Practice not engaging with the

content of your thoughts and redirecting your attention to the body each time you're captured by thought.

Breathe naturally, and notice how sensations just come and go. Start to taste the Stillness beneath all the sensations and all the thoughts.

When you're ready to move, form an intention to come back to this Stillness again and again, as often as you remember.

A LOOK AHEAD

In this opening chapter, I've tried to relate to you the personal way in which Life invited me to transform. The more I give myself to the process, the more it reveals how infinite our human-divinity is. In that vein, I've also offered a contemporary expression of the good news: Divine Love abounds, and we humans are gifted with time in order to become beings of Eternity. Practically speaking, there are principles of transformative practice that help increase our capacity to know joy.

In chapter two, I explore different aspects of Intelligence. This section is an orientation to the human being through the body, heart, and mind as distinct modes of knowing. In other words, we're not just going to learn new ideas in this book. Although the concepts, theories, and frameworks are robust, they're really only one part of the equation. The intention is to increase our being by more fully embodying all of what we are. We will engage the intellectual faculties meaningfully. But we'll also work with waking up the heart and experiencing life through the heart's characteristic perception of *Oneness*. We'll spend time in the physical body—an instrument of intelligence that learns by moving and by doing. By embodying more of our fullness, we'll come to appreciate at a deeper level the way the Spirit communicates to us through distinct centers of Intelligence.

In chapter three, I write about how to steady the mind. When we use the word *mind* in modern English, we often associate it with thinking—cognition, reason, and intellect. When I say "mind," I'm including this conventional meaning, but I'm also pointing to awareness itself. That is, who are we at a level deeper than any thought can penetrate? As a provisional metaphor, this practice is like polishing a mirror. The cleaner the mirror, the more clearly it can reflect objects. When awareness is stable and bright, we become more sensitive to refined spiritual energies, subtle graces that normally go undetected in ordinary life. In fact, so-called ordinary experience reveals itself to be quite extraordinary when we're fully present. But we tend not to notice the divine display because we're so hypnotized by the next thought, the next text message, the next banner ad. When we bounce around on the surface level of thought and emotion, we are blinded to the deeper spiritual realities that literally constitute human-divine life. Chapter three, then, is all about how to train awareness and use the undivided mind as a tool to more fully behold Sacred Reality. It is an exercise in thinning the veil.

I have dedicated chapter four entirely to the heart. Again, *heart* can be as confusing a word as *mind*. With *heart*, I'm not just referring to the physical organ—though that is important—and I'm not especially interested in talking about feelings, though I will discuss them a bit. We'll learn to relate to the heart as a sensitive spiritual instrument that opens doors to new mansions. For most of us, these capacities remain latent. We need to learn to see beneath the surface activity of emotions and into the depths of what the heart really knows and how big it really is. Through the heart, we can learn to express our spiritual gifts more fully and learn how to use those gifts in service of others.

As we get deeper into the process of transformation, we realize that in certain moments in life, we're very high functioning. We're naturally at our best. In other moments, we're less so. We start to notice, to our chagrin, where we're most wounded and fear-based. In a Christian sense, we see where we're caught in the thrall of sin. In chapter five I examine the woundedness of our humanity. I'll invite you to get honest about where you are most wounded and, therefore, low functioning. Together, we'll ask: "Where in life am I not showing up as my higher self, as my divine essence?" We'll take time to really be with this tenderness, to invite healing and more Grace into the process. It is a practice of allowing our core vulnerabilities, our most wounded humanity, to be redeemed and brought back into the Light.

Chapter six deals with key themes in adult development. As humans, we've always had an intuition about our own development. We see children grow right before our eyes and have created societies that help children grow into (hopefully) happy and contributing adults. But it has only been in the last several decades that we've brought to bear the scientific method on the nuances of not just child development but adult development. We've learned through research and studies that adults don't simply plateau at a certain age when their bodies are fully grown and their brains fully formed. We're learning that there are at least as many distinct stages and themes in adulthood as we'd previously recognized in childhood.

These themes of adult development, or what have been called "stages of faith" in religious contexts, profoundly color the way we make meaning in life. They give shape to who we understand ourselves to be as well as how we make sense of Divine Reality, faith, religion, and every other question that concerns us as disciples of Christ. We'll see from different perspectives how life might look when viewed through different lenses, different stages of development.

In chapter seven, we'll integrate all the previous learning and add the capstone: personal growth *is* collective growth. In spiritual development, we're never simply out to perfect the self. Stated even more strongly, there is no self that is not already connected to a living network of divine others. The more our hearts awaken to Sacred Reality, the more we come to the moral recognition that we are all responsible for one another. Our chief concern all along—whether we realized it or not—was actually to help redeem all of humanity and Creation.

I'll add as a coda to this opening chapter that if you're reading this book on your own, you might consider finding someone to take the journey with you. Reading has a tendency to remain up in the head, sealed up in the privatized domain of one's personal thoughts. Finding someone to read this book with or even to share impressions with along the way can help you start practicing divine communion right now.

Chapter 2

Increase in Being

IMAGINE YOU'RE SITTING at your desk, eagerly raising your hand, hoping your teacher calls on you to tell the rest of the class the capital of North Dakota (it's Bismarck, by the way). You get the answer right and pleasant sensations fill your whole body as you beam with pride before your admiring classmates. The bell for recess suddenly clangs, and you bound out onto the playground for a much needed romp after flexing your brain muscles all morning long.

Ten years later, your college professor asks if anyone can describe the distinct literary qualities of the postmodern period. Once again, you raise your hand with gusto, dazzling the other students with your knowledge of deconstruction, Marxist theory, and the context-bound nature of all human knowledge. Your professor is visibly impressed. Some of your classmates even look a bit envious. Once again, pleasant sensations arise in your body. Only now, there is no recess bell that follows. No frivolous playtime structured into your day. During the course of your formation as a WEIRD (that is, Western, educated, industrialized, rich, and democratic[1]) pupil, your body has slowly faded into the background of your awareness. Whether you realize it or not, you've come to believe that the thinking mind is both the locus of your identity and the source of all reliable knowledge.

If you're reading this book—or if you read books at all—you were likely significantly socialized to rely on the mind for the answers to life's most important questions. Things were not always this way, however, nor do they need to remain this way. There are faculties of knowing apart from the thinking mind, spiritual potentials that we are not making full use of.

We tend to associate growth and transformation with learning new ideas and taking new perspectives, which both imply intellectual understanding. This association is not a bad thing by any means. The intellectual center of the human being, or the mind's knowing, is supremely important. But in my approach, it is not more important than *other kinds of knowing*.

When we survey the wisdom traditions of the world, we see a pattern again and again. For millennia, humans have recognized and honored different ways of knowing. The Zen Buddhist sits in meditative absorption, stable as a mountain yet flowing like a river all at once. Both body and mind merge with nature and come to express the spontaneity of Creation itself. In the meantime, the Sufi chants the names of Allah, whirls in ecstasy, dying like a moth to the flame in devotion to Ultimate Reality. As the heart awakens, the Sufi no longer makes any distinction between lover, Beloved, and Love itself. Even the Prophet Joseph Smith emphasized an integrative style of wisdom when he said we must first "study it out" in our mind, and only then will the Lord cause our hearts to burn (Doctrine and Covenants 9:8–9). We may conclude that different traditions emphasize unique ways of knowing and cultivate diverse spiritual experiences as a result.

We know from our Western upbringing that the mind's ways of knowing and understanding are important. But in this chapter I want to offer some new language and practice regarding all of our faculties of Intelligence, classically expressed as body, heart, and mind.

I'm bringing attention to our different "centers of intelligence"[2] early on because if I don't, I know how tempting it can be to turn a book like this into a litany of ideas. Many of us, including myself, have a habit of feeding on new concepts without letting the nutrients really enter the bloodstream. When we locate Intelligence in the thinking mind alone, fixated on thought forms, the heart languishes and the body withers. We get so caught up in concepts that we lose touch with the body's pulsating rhythms, the heart's sympathetic resonance with "the hymn of the universe."[3] We forget what it's like to rest in the simple feeling of being, born of the Divine Light moment to moment.

Though we're not simply trading in new ideas in this book, new ideas remain vitally important. Ideas that are aligned with correct principles and divine patterns help us shift our perception. They can help us channel energy and attention in new ways. If all goes well, new perspectives will percolate deep into the heart and body. The substance of our being transforms, and how we show up in the world—our conduct—shifts. That's the real acid test: If our conduct is *spontaneously* becoming more selfless, more virtuous, we can trust we're headed in the right direction. On the other hand, if we find ourselves exerting great effort to improve our conduct and trying to be "good," we're probably stuck in our ideas of goodness and failing to *convert* at a deeper level. In short, my experience is that when we give attention to all the modes of Intelligence—body, heart, and mind—transformation happens naturally.

President Dallin H. Oaks gave an insightful general conference address[4] at the turn of the century on a related note. In his talk, he teaches that in the gospel of Jesus Christ, we're not just given the opportunity to learn something new, we're given the opportunity to *become something new.* Becoming something new goes far beyond affirming a belief in certain ideas. Becoming is a process of *conversion*, which entails "a profound change in nature."

Maurice Nicoll, a Scottish neurologist, psychiatrist, and modern teacher of Christian wisdom, pithily summarizes the path of becoming: "As one's level of being increases, receptivity to higher meaning increases. As one's being decreases, the old meanings return."[5]

Nicoll isn't saying that "higher meaning" involves increasingly complex interpretations of scripture and doctrine. He's using "meaning" in its broadest sense. In terms of Latter-day Saint theology, I would suggest that he's referring to Light, Truth, and Intelligence. Growing into the full stature of our divinity, we understand greater degrees of *meaning*, or Truth, that remain obscure to us when we "see in a mirror dimly" (1 Corinthians 13:12, ESV).

If we're growing in the sense I'm describing here, we're not just learning new ideas and increasing our fund of knowledge. *Our very being is increasing.* As our being increases, our receptivity to greater Intelligence, new qualities of meaning, become more plain to us. And then, when we *collapse* back into the "small self"—the natural man or woman—with all its vices and afflictions, the higher meaning that Nicoll points to, this ocean of Beingness and Light, appears veiled. I say "appears" veiled because it's not as if the ocean of Light and Infinite Intelligence goes anywhere (where could it go?). But our availability to perceiving and experiencing *more of* our *Divine Wholeness* collapses. In this light, we could say that all authentic spiritual practice involves increasing our sensitivity and receptivity to more being, more Light—to higher meaning.

Let's try an exercise. Reflect for a moment on the last time you made a really important life decision—a career move, a new relationship, whether to have kids, where to live. Notice when you needed to make that important decision, when you needed to really know some thing, where did you naturally channel your attention? That is, *from what part of your being* did you orient most of the time?

I ask this question because we all have different habits and styles of knowing. Some of us instinctively stay close to the thinking mind. We look up to thought to wrestle with life's difficult questions. Even if thinking is not our native style, we've certainly been taught to rely on thought in order to know something. But many of us, when we're invited to notice, we realize: "Actually, when I really need to know something, I rely on what I know to be true in my heart." How do I feel about changing careers? Should I offer some advice to my teenager or hang back and respect their space?

The knowing of the heart is a totally distinct quality from the knowing of the mind. We sense and know through the body in still another way. Of course, in real life, our knowing tends to be a blend of all three of these styles. But whatever your go-to style may be, we all have the opportunity to grow and expand. If you're a "head type," so to speak, you have the opportunity to direct more awareness through the intelligence of the heart. If you're a "heart type," maybe you would do well to get outside and move around in nature to work through one of life's conundrums. And if you're an intuitive who prefers to go with your gut, you might try rigorously thinking through some of your nonlinear impressions to see if they actually pass muster.

Whatever our unique style, the invitation now and always is to grow across all dimensions of Intelligence so that we're steadily increasing our being, we're becoming more receptive to higher meaning. I've found that when we pay attention in this new way, the Spirit has greater access to and through all of our faculties. This, in turn, leads to higher-quality decisions and more inspired action more of the time.

In the following sections I'd like to go into a little more detail on our different modes of Intelligence—both their distinctive gifts as well as what might get in the way of enjoying these gifts.

JOURNAL/REFLECT:

When you want to know something, where do you most often look from? From the sensations and intuition of the body? From the intelligence of the heart? The keenness of the intellect? Notice your habits of paying attention in this way and hold an intention to stretch into new ways of knowing.

THE BODY'S KNOWING

In the domain of the body, the Episcopalian priest and wisdom teacher par excellence Cynthia Bourgeault gives the advice to "follow your feet." What she means is that sometimes our body literally moves us in a certain direction that we not only didn't anticipate through the mind or the heart but we couldn't have anticipated through any other mode of Intelligence.

One of the most powerful and consequential experiences of my life happened one Sunday morning when out of nowhere, I felt the urge in my body to walk down the street and attend a sacrament meeting. It was as if my body was craving a nutrient I hadn't eaten in a long time. In fact, it had been almost twenty years since I'd *eaten* the sacrament.

When I entered the well-worn chapel, the smell of the wooden pews and old hymnals was rising up like incense. In fact, I remember feeling panic in my body at first—deep somatic memory of challenging experiences I'd had at church when I was very young. But I moved through it. When I finally sat down, I could feel the light of sunrise streaming in through the stained glass windows, as palpable as a loving parent's undivided attention on me. My mind was confused. I recall thinking, "What am I doing at church?" But an *inner knowing* told me I'd come home.

Yielding to different ways of knowing in different moments of life is another way of saying, "Live prayerfully—walk softly and give God plenty of ways to get through to you." There is always an abundance of divine guidance available at any given time. Sometimes we're just tuned in to the wrong channel. I'm so grateful that I followed my feet that morning. Confusing as it felt at the time, my body knew what my soul needed in a way my mind didn't even know it didn't know.

In light of the territory we're about to explore, I want to invite you to slow down and breathe.

Give yourself a moment to drop into sensation more fully by taking some nice, deep breaths. Let your breath fan the flames of sensation and amplify what you feel throughout the entire physical body.

For the moment, let go of any mental content. Anything that's been swirling around in your mind today, or this week, you can let it be in the background of your awareness. You don't have to stop thoughts, like turning off a spigot. You can simply have an intention to background thoughts, assigning them less importance for the time being.

Feel *through* the body. And notice how I word that. I'm not asking you to visualize the body but to actually gather awareness in the body and feel sensation *from the inside*. Notice how you feel in the moment. Hold an intention to remain in sensation as you continue reading.

This is not an easy practice. I mentioned that most of us have spent a lifetime revving up the endless thoughts that pass through awareness. To take our foot off the gas pedal of the thinking mind and start to coast to a standstill is a new skill for many of us. Not only that, but what I've found by working deeply in the body is that we all tend to have a lot of hangups here. We tend to have very mixed feelings about more fully inhabiting the body. I don't think it's an exaggeration to call our collective condition one of "body loathing," whether we're aware of it or not.

BODY LOATHING

Body loathing is not extrinsic to the Christian tradition itself. In fact, I would argue that in Christianity, some of our deepest misgivings towards the physical body have crystallized into doctrines that have all too often gone unexamined.

I want to offer a few salient examples that I believe exacerbate the anxiety we tend to feel towards the body. In the process, I hope we can start to come into a new relationship with this aspect of our divinity *right now*.

The Apostle Paul advised the early Christians not to marry if they were unmarried: "But if they cannot contain, let them marry: for it is better to marry than to burn" (1 Corinthians 7:9, KJV). Translators who came later, perhaps uneasy with the threat of hellfire, modified it to such phrases as "it's better to marry than to burn *with lust*" (NLT;[6] emphasis added). Whether we're burning in hell for our fornicating or merely burning with lust, for my purposes, it amounts to the same thing. There's a strong message here that the body is a problem to be dealt with. What Paul doesn't write in this verse is as telling as what he does write. He does not take time to praise the beautiful, creative, and divine nature of sexual energy. He does not qualify his statement by reminding his fold that the body is intrinsically holy, though fallible. Instead, he expresses something to the effect of, "Ideally, you don't have any sex at all. But if you *must* have sex, make sure you do it in wedlock."

It's not just our view of the body that has been tainted. Our relationship to the physical world itself has been shaped in surprising ways by Greco-Roman culture and philosophy. For example, the early Christian movement incorporated the idea of Platonic forms, which says there is a perfect world "out there" in contrast to the deficient (and "fallen") world we live in. (Many centuries later, Joseph Smith revealed that the Fall of Adam was in fact necessary to make possible a fullness of joy. In the restored gospel's telling, physicality is not a fall from anything. It is a glorious ascent. The body is not fallen—it is the god and the goddess in embryo.)

As a final example of the story, metaphor, and language that affect our relationship to the body as Christians, I point to Christ's Ascension after His Resurrection. In the Apostle's Creed, it reads that "he ascended into heaven and is seated at the right hand of God the Father almighty."[7] I can't help but see the significant Hellenistic influence in this very scripture—this idea that Christ is born, He lives and dies, and in the opportune moment, He moves *up and out*. This is the mantra of a body-loathing Christianity—"up and out." Christ *ascends* to His Father's throne, up and away from this fallen world, this world of shadows.

Perhaps a less appreciated detail in the scriptural record is that before Christ goes "up and out," He goes *down and through*: "For as Jonah was in the belly of the great fish for three days and three nights, so will the Son of Man be in the heart of the earth for three days and three nights" (Matthew 12:40, NLT). We mustn't ignore the fact that at the moment of Christ's death, He first goes straight to the "heart of the earth." That is, "he that ascended up on high, as also he descended below all things, in that he comprehended all things, that he might be in and through all things, the light of truth" (Doctrine and Covenants 88:6).

This revealed scripture clearly states that the transformative process for Christ (and we can suppose it is the same for ourselves) isn't just a movement of "up and out." It's not a matter of passing the test in a body then flitting off to the "real world" of spirit. Exactly as much as there is an "up and out," a *transcendence* in the spiritual journey, there is a moving "down and through," an *immanence*, into the heart of the earth and the very heart of matter. If Christ is *living*, it is not only *beyond* matter where He[8] resides but in and through all matter, redeeming all of Creation—from the rocks, to the plants, to the animals, to the entire human family.

Until now I haven't even mentioned death and dying. How comfortable can we be in this "temple" that biologically starts to break down in our mid-twenties? Disease, chronic pain, the inevitable loss of everything we've ever come to love in this world—they are all integral to the experience of having an earthly body. It's no wonder we spend so much time in our heads, blunting the intensity of embodied reality. To be fully embodied is to consciously participate in grief, loss, sickness, and ultimately death.

And yet Christ teaches us that true life comes in and through death. Life and death are One in Sacred Reality. Therefore, to catalyze the process of spiritual transformation, we do not escape *from* the body. We escape *into* it. So that we too come to comprehend life, death, and everything in between.

MEDITATION
Entering into God's Rest

FULFILLMENT OF OUR DIVINE BEING

Now that we've become a little more sensitive to common hang-ups with the body, let's return to the body's unique Intelligence. When we fully inhabit the body in all its aches, pains, pleasures, and glory, we realize that *we can learn and know profound spiritual truths through the body that we can't learn any other way.* The body is not just the seat of our lower nature, as Paul would sometimes have it. It is a fulfillment of our divine being and has its own unique way of learning from the Reality in which "we live, and move, and have our being" (Acts 17:28, KJV).

My son is not quite two years old. We play a little game at the church a few doors down. He makes his way up a fairly steep slope on the church lawn, and as he's walking up the hill, I say, "One, two, three, fall back!" After I say "fall back," he does just that—he flops backwards, without looking, as though he were going to land in a mound of down feathers. Of course, I'm right there to catch him, and every time I do, he squeals with delight as he gazes up into the sky. In and through his body, he's learning *trust*. He's too young to make a concept of it, but he knows in his body when he hears my voice that if he falls back, if he trusts the voice, it's going to be delightful. He'll let go into something bigger than he is and learn through repetition that there is a basic goodness to life that he can trust. When he falls, Life itself is going to catch him.

I have my own preferred ritual for learning through the body, one that has animated my spiritual life for many years now. It's the practice of "still sitting." Note that *still sitting* and *meditation* are sometimes synonymous terms. However, the former emphasizes the stillness of the body for prolonged periods of time more than anything one does with one's mind during the practice. In profound ways, this somatic approach to spiritual practice continues to teach me about the Divine Life.

For me, the body held in stillness is the ultimate gesture of "I will drink this cup." The practice is so simple: Sit on the ground with a straight spine. Kneeling is good too. Let everything else be soft. Whatever arises—thought, sensation, feeling—*be that*. Fully join with it so that there is absolutely no separation between you and the experience. In the moments when I want the cup to pass, when I don't want to feel the pain of what I'm feeling, I hold an intention to be *willing*, to fully receive what the Sacred has ordained for me to experience.

What I've learned through my body practicing stillness over the years is that when I am relaxed, openhearted, and *willing enough*, moment-to-moment experience is consecrated. Everything takes on a tinge of the Holy. By sitting still, I let go of the fantasy that one day things will be better. I stop looking to escape into yesterday or tomorrow and open up to the Fullness of what is here *right now*. In other words, *I neither toil nor spin*. Each time I stretch out my legs, stand up and reenter the flow of daily life, I can better connect to the still point at the center of my being, around which everything turns, like the eye of a storm.

The physical body and world make possible all the most exquisite qualities of the kingdom. Pondering on my son's ritual, which I described above, how could he possibly learn trust in this way without a body? How could *trust* as we know it in our earthly estate even exist without the body? To trust, we need to first experience separation. Only then can we practice giving ourselves in sacred union to Powers beyond ourselves. When the Muslim touches her head to the ground in prostration, she bodies forth *surrender to God*. When a child learns to fold his arms in the chapel, with his body as instrument, he gives reverence for God a tangible form.

The body's knowing, of course, is not limited to religious contexts. I remember the first real wave I ever caught on a surfboard—in a small Basque town that is the stuff of postcards. The power of the wave pulled me into the curl and propelled me forward, sending a thrill through my body that took my breath away. I was moving forward and backwards simultaneously. I was weightless and substantial all at once. For a moment, I entered God's dance—*the play of opposites*. Another image just now comes to me as a sleep-deprived parent: My daughter, who is four months old, lights up in her bassinet when she sees me or my wife come into the room. Her unbridled life energy animates her legs in a happy dance like water gushing out of a garden hose in spasms. Without those chubby, supple human legs, there can be no fullness of joy.

What I want to instill is that through movement, through gesture, through intuition deeper than any thought can comprehend, the body expresses the rhythms of the cosmos and gives outward form to the infinite qualities of the Divine. We can learn to trust this movement and go for the ride.

THOUGHT EXPERIMENT:

(Feel free to journal as well as do some walking meditation with this prompt.)

What if this very body, this very world were already heaven? Rather than relating to this life as a test to get somewhere better, what if you treated this very moment as the better place you were hoping to get to? You've already arrived. This is it.

How would you act differently if this were the case? In what way do you start to perceive things differently when you take this to be true?

THE HEART'S KNOWING

The next distinct way of knowing I'd like to explore is *kardial intelligence,*[9] or the intelligence of the heart. Saint John of the Cross wrote in "The Dark Night of the Soul,"

> On that glad night,
> in secret, for no one saw me,
> nor did I look at anything,
> with no other light or guide
> than the one that burned in my heart.[10]

INCREASE IN BEING | 33

In this poem, beloved to mystics the world over, the "glad night" is a metaphor for union with the Divine. I especially love the words "with no other light or guide." Often, habitually, the light and the guide of human life is the thinking mind. So often we're looking closely at our thoughts, trying to understand something, to know something. The mind loves to have answers; it hates to *not know*. Yet Saint John, a master of prayer and contemplation in our Christian tradition, points in this stanza to a new quality of Intelligence that reveals itself when we are willing to not know. When we are willing to travel without "light or guide"—that is, the conventional support of intellectual understanding—a knowing beyond any understanding burns within us.

How did the two disciples on the road to Emmaus finally recognize the risen Christ? It wasn't by the eye of flesh they discerned Him. He walked with them, entered their home, and they still did not see. In a flash of recognition, as Christ broke bread and spoke a blessing, they suddenly knew something *through* their hearts that their minds did not believe was possible: "Did not our heart burn within us, while he talked with us by the way, and while he opened to us the scriptures?" (Luke 24:32, KJV). Poetry and scriptures such as these point beautifully to the reality of the heart's knowing.

I have a personal story about the heart. It comes from the very first time I decided I was going to sit still and try to intentionally work with my mind. I remember the meditation period feeling punishingly long and being physically painful. Mentally and emotionally, I had a heightened sense of how unwilling I was to just sit in the messiness of my life without distraction. I don't know how long I sat that particular day, but it felt like the length of a three-hour movie that goes nowhere enjoyable.

But at some point during that yawning span, I felt a shock of recognition. If I had to put it into words, it was like an awesome taste of *Oneness*. It was direct intuition—a *felt sense* of unity, not merely an idea. In hindsight, I think my mind gave out due to utter exhaustion from trying to focus for so long. It's like when you do as many push-ups as you possibly can then try to do just one more. But your arms are like jelly, and it's not going to happen. My mind had become jelly-like, and just then, the "eye of the heart" was able to open, if only tentatively. I was perceiving, I was knowing *through* the heart, and what I suddenly *knew* was that I was seamlessly One with all of life, and that I was cared for infinitely. I only caught a glimpse, but that glimpse made a lasting impression.

It took me years after that moment to really cultivate and refine the insight I'd had. In time, I came to see more clearly the way in which the intellect—the mind's knowing—knows by way of thought forms. It knows by detecting shades of difference and by making distinctions. Gregory Bateson famously said that information "is a difference which makes a difference." Bateson's insight points directly to the logic of the mind: it sees through difference, even creates difference, and revels in that difference. Difference to the mind, in a religious sense, is the multiplicity of Infinite Divine Form. Everything we know by way of the mind, we know because *this is not that*. You're over there, and I'm over here. Night is night, and day is day. Life is life, and death is death. They're different. At least, different in the mind's knowing.

But the heart works by a totally distinct perceptual reality. Whereas the mind divides, dissects, and analyzes, the heart unifies, embraces, and *resonates with*—akin to notes resonating in a rich musical chord. In the moment of meditation I described above, I fell into the heart's knowing. My heart was resonating with everything, everywhere, it seemed. For a brief moment, I felt "me" as a wave rising up from the boundless ocean. This type of experience happens when, in Eastern Orthodox terms, we "put the mind in the heart." The heart naturally knows through a warm, resonant, loving Oneness with all that is. Most people find it to be supremely beautiful when they experience this. Beautiful and also *moral*. When we experience unity, we naturally want to take care of Sacred Creation the same way we take care of our own feet or our own eyeballs. It's that tender.

Note that what I'm referring to is not some special experience that only spiritually gifted people have access to. It is a dimension of human-divinity that is always here, right now, for all of us. In a given moment, we can slow down, relax, and *put the mind in the heart*. If we feel frenetic or anxious, if we feel alienated from God or lost in the world, we can learn to open the eye of the heart and see what the world looks like from a place of undividedness.

One major challenge to developing kardial intelligence, I've found, is that often, unconsciously, we tend to avoid feeling what's in our heart at a given time. Why? Without oversimplifying the matter, I'd say that the heart is just so exquisitely sensitive. We actually feel so much through the heart naturally that when we're totally open to the experience, it can frighten us. It can overwhelm us. Think about it—the mind knows what it knows by dividing the world into manageable categories and concepts. From the mind's point of view, the "self" is safely separate from other selves and free to go about its own way. We can deal with one sliver of a manageable reality at a time. Not so with the heart. When we're truly embodied at a heart level, our conventional ego boundaries soften, even dissolve. We realize we're not who we *thought* we were. We're much *bigger*. What's more, as we realize we're not just a small, separate, isolated self anymore, we'll have a moral reckoning sooner or later. We realize we're responsible, on some level, for all of Creation.

In a timeless literary passage, Fyodor Dostoevsky gives voice to this insight through his character Zossima in *The Brothers Karamazov*:

> My young brother asked forgiveness of the birds: it seems senseless, yet it is right, for all is like an ocean, all flows and connects; touch it in one place and it echoes at the other end of the world. Let it be madness to ask forgiveness of the

birds, still it would be easier for the birds, and for a child, and for any animal near you, if you yourself were more gracious than you are now, if only by a drop, still it would be easier. All is like an ocean, I say to you. Tormented by universal love, you, too, would then start praying to the birds, as if in a sort of ecstasy, and entreat them to forgive you your sin. Cherish this ecstasy, however senseless it may seem to people.[11]

To open up to the immensity of the heart's knowing requires us to humble ourselves in ways that cause the mind to recoil. It requires us to confront our pain as well as the fear that we will drown in the world's grief and sorrow if we open up to it. It asks us to take radical responsibility for the cost of our arising and to confess that every action we take, every thought we think, and feeling we feel "echoes at the other end of the world."

Seen in this way, it's understandable that we do not wish to open up to the realities of the heart's knowing all at once. In T. S. Eliot's words, it is "a condition of complete simplicity / (Costing not less than everything)."[12]

As a final clarification, it's important to understand that when we're talking about the knowing of the heart, it is a distinct terrain from Western culture's obsession with feeling intense feelings and pursuing individual passions. Not that there isn't a space in a healthy human life to feel intensely and to be engaged with our passions. There very much is. But to exercise the heart's latent capacities, we need to train ourselves to see through surface-level emotions into the heart's unsearchable depths.

From the perspective of transformative practice, the emotions cloud over the more subtle currents of Intelligence we can detect through the instrument of the heart. Like stirring up mud in a pond, our emotions risk obscuring the clarity of the heart's profound sensitivity and knowing. It's not so different from a chronically glutted mind that has no room for inspiration or creativity because it's so full of spam—random thoughts full of empty calories.

Pay close attention to St. John's words: "nor did I look at anything / with no other light or guide." He is speaking of the heart's pure knowing—deeper than any emotion, more subtle than any thought, a form of highly concentrated Love and Light. This Intelligence is the spiritual territory we're given to master in our human-divinity.

PRACTICE:

Whenever you remember to remember, notice when life starts to feel too heady or too intellectual or disconnected or alienating. Just learn to notice this feeling of disconnect in your being. Then . . .

Take a good, deep breath.

Feel your feet on the ground. Let your belly be soft and your spine straight.

Relax through the heart. Put the mind in the heart. That is, bring your awareness to the inside of sensation in and around the physical heart and rest there for a few moments. Start to get a feel for knowing from the heart.

Just notice. What does the world feel like now? It might not always be pleasant when seeing from the heart. But it will be true.

THE MIND'S KNOWING

We now turn to the intellectual faculties, the mind's knowing. I realize that in my teaching I sometimes give short shrift to the glories of mind. I think I do this because the status of the mind is already so elevated in our culture. I'm afraid if I offer more praise, I risk perpetuating the imbalance I see in modern life. Nevertheless, allow me to give credit where credit is due. Without the genius of the intellect, humanity remains endarkened, embedded in a blooming buzz of perception with no means to connect the dots to higher order principles. We fail to see the divine patterning through which Sacred Reality takes form. Without the mind's knowing, there is no true understanding. We stare blankly at what's before us, failing to imagine the adjacent possible. That is, we cannot see in our mind's eye what this moment might yet become.

In a related insight, William Shakespeare poignantly writes that there is "special / providence in the fall of a sparrow."[13] Because the mind grasps difference so keenly, it reveals to us the *uniqueness* of every created thing. *This* sparrow is precious because it is different from *that* sparrow. *You* are precious because there is no being like you in all of the cosmos. As the mind's knowing sensitizes us to uniqueness, to preciousness, our heart opens to a vision of the Divine Nature that we all share. Shakespeare's verse is yet another example that the centers of Intelligence work best when they work in unison.

In full appreciation of the mind's knowing, I do want to express some caution. I've mentioned that through cultural reinforcement, we tend to prize the intellectual faculties above others. René Descartes sums up our post-Enlightenment attitudes when he wrote, "I think, therefore I am."[14] It follows that if I don't think, I don't exist. And therefore the essence of my very being is thinking.

Notwithstanding Descartes's profound accomplishments, this statement is rather lopsided from a wisdom perspective. Thinking is at best a portion of the fullness of our being. What we're interested in is a fullness of joy—full embodiment.

That said, we don't want to commit the opposite error of shunning the thinking mind and its capacities. In many spiritual communities nowadays, it's a popular notion that thinking is an enemy to spirituality. This perspective is a case of a good insight gone too far.

INCREASE IN BEING | 39

Maybe a more moderate way to state the case is that in some moments, the thinking mind is just not the right tool for the job. Sometimes, the thinking mind helps us discern exactly what is needed. Other times, it can only get in our way. The crux is to learn to freely access different kinds of intelligence as needed. Growing into our full stature involves an ever-deepening integration of *all* of who we are.

PITFALLS OF THE THINKING MIND

The most pernicious pitfall of all is not the thinking mind itself, but our relationship to it. We hold deep cultural beliefs that the mind's knowing is the gold standard of intelligence. Human beings in the modern world often believe that intellectual understanding is more reliable than any other kind of knowing. For example, we're so culturally invested in the belief that the "scientific" and rational mind will eventually know all there is to know that we ignore that our base of knowledge continues to shift under our feet. Dr. Charles Burwell, dean of Harvard Medical School from 1935 to 1949, famously said to his students: "Half of what we are going to teach you is wrong, and half of it is right. Our problem is that we don't know which half is which."[15] As powerful as the mind is, it is always limited by how much it can see in a given moment and how much of the Whole it can take in. This being the case, let us never forget that knowledge will always be expanding in surprising ways. A thousand years ago we "knew" that the sun revolved around the earth. Today, many a jaded modern "knows" that matter is all that exists in the universe—there is no spirit. What will we "know" a thousand years from today? To relate to the thinking mind as a stakeholder in the health of Zion rather than as the supreme leader of an infallible empire is an important step we can all take toward sanity.

Abstraction is another blessing-curse that comes with the intellect. Our powers of abstraction are formidable as human beings. By abstraction, I mean the capacity to reduce complex reality to ideas, theories, and mental models. On one hand, this ability is a profound blessing to humanity. For example, using the language of mathematics and the means of modern technology, collectively we were able to send people to the moon in 1969—a feat that previously seemed unthinkable. The flip side to abstraction, though, is profound disembodiment—*excarnation*. Our ideas, our wishes, our dreams at no point touch down on the earth, and in the end, they can become a gross form of escapism and denial. It is not hard to connect the dots between our current ecological crisis and the human power of intellectual abstraction. Chasing a certain vision—in this case, unlimited economic expansion and material wealth—we've lost touch with our own bodies as well as with the earth herself who sustains us.

Another liability of the thinking mind is the prison of repetition. As all things in Creation, the intellect is susceptible to habit. That is, it's difficult to think new thoughts and relatively easy to rehearse old ones. If I've grown up in an environment that teaches me to think that the restored gospel is superior to other religions, my thoughts will organize around these familiar grooves and blind me to the gifts of other spiritual traditions. Just as a physical body can grow stiff and weak without proper exercise and stretching, the mind readily closes in on itself, defensive of all its cherished beliefs as well as resistant to allowing new kinds of inspiration to enter.

On a related note, and somewhat counterintuitively, the mind is slow. Of all the centers of Intelligence, the thinking mind is actually the most plodding. Again, this concept flies in the face of our cultural prejudice that the mind is *quick* and *agile*. In fact, when we look closer at what really high-quality thinking is, we see that it is actually *thoughtless*. That is why it is said in the tradition of Advaita Vedanta that "real thinkers don't think." Bursts of insight and inspiration show up spontaneously in awareness; *only after the fact* does the mind go about making sense of it, explaining it, organizing the Intelligence into something knowable and useful to us in the human world. To be sure, this translation process, from unborn Light into words and concepts, is extremely important. It's a means of building pathways, even super highways across which more Light and Intelligence can travel more readily. But the roads are not the destination. Working out new ideas, concepts, hypotheses in a methodical, linear fashion is an indispensable part of human growth and becoming. But if all we have is the thinking mind—no openness to the heart, to the body's knowing, to awareness itself—the mind tends to loop on itself, driving endless circles on well-worn lanes. We get stuck in the mind's traffic jams and can never find an exit that will take us to the beach.

EMBODIED AT ALL LEVELS

We've been exploring the distinct modes of knowing that we all have access to as human beings. In doing so, we're expanding what it means to "learn" in significant ways. We're also expanding our sense of *how* to learn and, therefore, how to truly transform. The body through movement, through gesture realizes profound spiritual truths that are elusive to the heart and mind. When the heart is awake and clear, we learn about unity and our Oneness with all that is Sacred. The intellect celebrates multiplicity and makes empowering distinctions. Spirit, or Intelligence, animates all these diverse ways of knowing and more.

As you inhabit more of yourself, the more you carve out greater depths of being in yourself, the more you will become receptive and sensitive to higher meanings and new realities. These new realities, these *mansions*, are full of Grace, Power, and Dignity. And they are right here, not somewhere else. The kingdom of heaven is closer than close.

Most of us don't abide in this state of Grace as often as we could. We *collapse* many times a day into compulsive thinking, bouts of anxiety, and waves of boredom. But just this is the practice: to note when we collapse then practice opening up into greater Fullness, again and again. Mortality exercises us in this way. Our sense of self contracts and expands just like a muscle when we're working out at the gym. We need this exercise—Spirit incarnating as matter and matter waking up more fully as Spirit—to grow into divine beings. In this sense, Sacred Reality uses time to create beings who can bear the Light of Eternity.

As we practice, we learn that to remain awake through all of our faculties requires extra effort, at least at first. We need to get used to the new intensity, the higher energy state of occupying all of our being at once. To sleep in time requires less *being* than to wake in Eternity.

Some of my friends and colleagues have written beautifully about this topic. Their words are descriptive of the abundant life we intend and yearn for as human beings and as disciples of Christ. "Embodiment is occurring at all the levels of our incarnate being. We can be embodied physically, energetically, emotionally, mentally, and spiritually, but to be truly embodied is to be embodied at all levels, in our wholeness."[16] In this sense, we can say that *embodiment* is happening all the time. But how embodied are we? Most of us have no problem being "mentally embodied." But if we're chronically caught up in thought, what promptings are we missing in the vitality of the body? What revelations go undetected in the heart's sacred silence?

We all have the spiritual capacity to be even more fully embodied. Arguably, this ability is what we're here to practice as human beings—to receive more Light and to grow "brighter and brighter until the perfect day" (Doctrine and Covenants 50:24). Let me offer an example to illustrate how this can play out in practical ways day to day.

Imagine you're with a friend, a loved one, a child—you're with another human being who is precious to you. This human being happens to be in the midst of a lot of suffering. As mammals, we have sensitive bodies and nervous systems that are wired to respond to one another. Being with another person during times of suffering inevitably brings up discomfort in our own body.[17] But if you're really comfortable inhabiting the body and willing to just be with the body as it is, the other person's pain, anxiety, heartbreak will not overwhelm you. In fact, by staying "grounded" in your own body and in touch with a sense of rest and calm, you offer unspoken support to this sacred other. You are like stable ground as they reel in pain and struggle to find their footing. I've had the privilege of working with many students over the years, and I find much of the time all that people really need is to feel a grounded, embodied presence—something to steady them as an earthquake shakes them to the core.

Other times when you're called to bear another's burden, the instrument of choice will be the heart. Oftentimes people don't need our advice or counsel. What they need is to feel *felt*. They need to feel like you're *resonating* with them. Like you know how they feel without even saying it. It so happens that this is the heart's genius. No thoughts, no judgments, not "my pain" or "your pain"—pain is just pain, and I am willing to feel it, wherever the apparent location of that pain happens to be. Research has shown that one of the most powerful things parents can do to form secure attachment with their children is to attune to them again and again, to give them the experience of being known and feeling felt.[18] Attunement is not only beneficial for children. We crave this same contact and intimacy from others throughout adulthood.

If we are willing to know through the heart when another person suffers, the chords of sorrow begin to sound, and we feel joy simply for the gift of playing in the same symphony. The next time you're offering somebody your support and this person seems inconsolable, remember that if you're willing to open up your heart and let those subtle strings vibrate, you will be adding your unique sound to the chords of cosmic joy and sorrow. Such is the sacred music of the heart center.

After grounding in the body and resonating with somebody's joy and sorrow through the heart, sometimes what people need in their suffering is your discernment. Sometimes they need words of wisdom—concrete advice. This discernment is the province of the intellectual center where we can see patterns and focus on what matters most, thus elevating us out of the quagmire of confusing emotions and impulses. "Can I offer you some feedback that might be hard to hear? I'm noticing that you often blame this person for your pain. But in blaming her, you make yourself a powerless victim. Does that ring true to you?" This is an example of the discriminating wisdom of the mind.

Hopefully you're starting to see by now that in the most ordinary of circumstances—just being with another human being—all our faculties are potentially online and in service of deeper relationship, deeper communion. If I'm stuck in my head, my loved ones remain unconsoled. I'm sitting here peddling my cheap advice (hoping to avoid my own suffering that their suffering activates in my body), and all they actually want is to feel that I'm fully here with them, undivided, undefended.

Other times, depending on my personality structures, I become so emotionally reactive to what other people are feeling, I lose my own sense of groundedness. It's as if I've heroically dived into the ocean to rescue the drowning swimmer only to need rescuing myself. In these moments, we all need dry ground. Our friends need to feel us breathing deep from our belly, stable, so they can fall apart, knowing that the groundless Ground will catch them in their fall.

Being awake and alive through all our different qualities of Intelligence allows us to show up more appropriately in the moment. Practicing in this way elevates us to *higher meaning* and deeper connection with ourselves and indeed with all beings. Being *truly embodied* is to channel more Life, Light, and Love in and through the world. In an ordinary way, it is how we build heaven right here, right now.

LIFE PRACTICE:

Be present with the people you love, and notice what you sense in a given moment: What is called for? A deep groundedness in the body and sense of peace? An open heart, resonating with another's experience? A keen mind, helping bring clarity and new perspectives to the situation? What about the quality of pure presence—open, receptive awareness? Likely, it's some combination of all these qualities that will be most healing.

Notice how you tend to show up in your relationships, and be curious about how you might bring more beingness, more presence to your encounters through the different centers of Intelligence.

MEDITATION
Embodying Fullness

FIRST INTERLUDE

Investigating the Self

UP TILL NOW, you might have wondered : "What's with all this talk about transformative practice? How is this any different than all the things I do in my religious life to grow and progress?" In a sense, there's no difference at all. Every experience we have in every moment of life transforms us.

Reading scripture is transformative practice. Praying is transformative practice. Temple worship, ministering, and even attending your local pancake breakfast sponsored by the stake is transformative practice. Potentially.

I say "potentially" because there are subtleties on the path that can trip us up and greatly limit our potential. Our contemporary understanding of transformation is becoming more sophisticated. In other words, we have new tools to investigate the "self."

For example, modern developmental science shows that our understanding of who we are evolves across a lifespan. As our sense of self matures, our motivation for acting the way we do matures with it. I'll describe this in greater detail in later chapters, but for the time being, it's important to bear in mind that the current self we take ourselves to be is not nearly as straightforward as we might have supposed.

To illustrate this, I want to offer a possible interpretation of one of Jesus's parables. In the story of the prodigal son, two sons have a birthright of, let's assume, unimaginable wealth. The younger son asks for his birthright prematurely and squanders it on a life of indulgence and profligate living. It's not until he's literally eating off the ground with pigs—symbolic of the lowest rung of society at the time—that he comes to himself and realizes all that he had. Having seen himself through new eyes, he returns home to seek his father's forgiveness.

Meanwhile, the older son has done everything he's ever been asked to do. In contemporary terms, we can imagine that he has a successful career, a respectable Church calling, and a fine-looking family. He serves his community dutifully and asks for nothing out of turn.

Suddenly, the rebellious younger brother returns home, and there is a grand celebration. "Kill the fatted calf! My son has returned at last," the father cries out jubilantly. But the older brother cannot find it in himself to be happy on the occasion. Why not?

I find the distinction between inner path and outer path to be helpful here. By *inner path*, I mean the process of clarifying our intentions that lead to action—irrespective of what our actions might look like to others. While the outer path calls us to engage in concrete behaviors and disciplines, the inner path calls for a steady eye on our more subtle motivations and desires—not what we do but *why* we do it. *From what depth in our being are we sourcing our actions?* In a perfect world, the outer path supports the inner path and vice versa. But in practice, the outer path can supplant genuine inner transformation. Spiritual life always risks becoming *performative*, not transformative.

From an inner-path perspective, the dutiful brother is stuck. He has become so fixated on duty and rule-following that he has fallen prey to his own spiritual pride—a telltale sign of lower nature. But he's doubly stuck because he can't see it. He mistakenly believes that if he does everything right and impeccably obeys the rules of the game, God will have no choice but to reward him. In other words, he tries to gain salvation by his own strength. He has mastered the outer path but failed to make forward progress on the inner path. He is truly the lost son among the two.

The so-called prodigal son, we could say, has arrived at the palace of wisdom through the path of excess. He realizes how poverty-stricken he truly is when following the appetite of his lower nature. Thoroughly exploring that spiritual cul-de-sac, he learns for himself—in the depth of his being—that there is a better way. His return to the father is a sign of genuine humility and repentance. He realizes nothing he does of himself can compare to God's generosity and the privilege of being a member in the kingdom.

The older son tries to perfect the self that isn't who he ultimately is—the false self—by obeying all the rules perfectly. The younger son realizes that he's not who he thought he was and chooses to die to his former self.

When we investigate the self, we realize that *what we do outwardly is far less important than the depth from which we source our motivation.* Acting from our lower nature, we can easily cloak ourselves in counterfeit righteousness, doing all the right things for all the wrong reasons. Acting from our higher nature, we are moved by Sacred Reality alone.

To realize that we are not who we thought we were and that *nothing* we do by way of conduct can guarantee us salvation is a frightening thing. In Christian terms, when we are honest about who we really are, we realize we're called to the cross. We're called to die to the one we thought we were. Again and again.

Our ideas and beliefs about who we are comprise a very small part of who we actually are. As we become embodied in our fullness, to paraphrase Joseph Smith, we are delivered from the "little narrow prison"[1] of the isolated thinking mind and its "scattered" language. No longer subsisting on the husks of an identity that was never ours to begin with, we come to feast on the bread of life.

Chapter 3

An Eye Single

HIGH STATES OF CONCENTRATION

Concentration can catalyze radical spiritual transformation.
When we're aware of how we're paying attention, we have more agency.
Complete concentration helps us express pure trust in God.

While these claims may not be the way we're accustomed to thinking about spiritual practice and growth, I invite you to explore these perspectives and see what might shift as a result.

In the Latter-day Saint tradition, we read an important call to concentration in Doctrine and Covenants: "And if your eye be single to my glory, your whole bodies shall be filled with light, and there shall be no darkness in you; and that body which is filled with light comprehendeth all things" (88:67).

While *glory* has a range of meaning in scripture—from God's importance to honor and majesty—here, it seems to point most directly to God's Presence. This scripture is inviting us to open our entire being to God's Presence. That sounds like a simple and powerful invitation. But if we sit still in silence for even a few moments, almost universally we discover that our minds are completely unruly. They are bouncing all over the place with wandering thoughts, regrets from the past and anxieties about the future. Despite our best efforts, it's difficult to keep our eye single.

I remember attending my first meditation retreat many years ago. It was ten days of silent meditation from sun up till sun down. The practice was exhausting for me, maybe most especially because it confronted me so many times with a sense of abject failure. No matter how hard I tried to focus, my mind seemed to go wherever it wanted to go. At the end of the retreat I remember hanging out in the open air and sunshine with other participants and reflecting on the grueling experience. One young man who was probably in his early twenties said pensively, "If I can't focus my mind here, how am I supposed to keep my mind focused in life and do the things I really want to do?" I remember the weight of his words to this day. The question for all of us becomes, "If we can't rest in Sacred Presence in this moment, undistracted, how can we fully consecrate our lives over an entire lifetime?" Will our days and our lives not be filled with distraction, just as our moments are?

A BRIEF HISTORY OF CONCENTRATION PRACTICES

Something I didn't appreciate until I was well into my own meditation practice is that what we call "meditation" nowadays has historically been much more a feature of daily life. Premodern life was more meditative by nature—more closely tied to the rhythms of the earth. Humans learned to ride these "waves of experience" into high states of concentration in order to access more refined aspects of Reality across the millennia.

Many historians point to the Vedas of the Hindu tradition when citing the first written record of meditation practice in human civilization. These were sacred mantras, syllables repeated deliberately to calm the mind and sensitize awareness to more refined levels of being. Conservatively, those practices were fully developed and in common use more than three thousand years ago.[1] And that is just what the written record indicates. Other anthropologists point to evidence that human beings were accessing spiritual experiences through high states of concentration as many as 65,000 years ago.[2] This fascinating history of meditation could constitute an entire volume of its own. But one key takeaway is this: humans have understood for a very long time the difference between our ordinary waking state and altered states of consciousness that give us heightened access to nourishing, enlivening, spiritual realities.

Christianity has cultivated its own style of meditation across the centuries. Many scholars have suggested that meditation practices from various traditions likely circulated on the Silk Road and significantly influenced the religious environment in which Jesus and his followers came of age.[3] But in the person of Jesus, those practices took a distinct turn. We don't know why the scriptures are so sparing in their description of Jesus's personal prayer life, though they do record that he often withdrew to solitary places in prayer (e.g., Luke 5:16; Mark 1:35). I'll have more to say about the practice of solitude as we proceed. But for now, I want to suggest that Jesus's life in its entirety was the quintessential example of Christian meditation, if we define meditation as perfect concentration or a giving of our entire being over to the Sacred.

Paul in his epistles later reflected this wisdom with the word *gnosis* to describe an intimate knowledge of God particular to those who love Him. The word connotes much more than an intellectual understanding of Deity. Rather, it suggests a whole-being encounter with Divine Reality, engaging all the centers of Intelligence we explored in the previous chapter. In later centuries, and through a cross-fertilizing of Neoplatonic philosophy and Judeo-Christian culture, Christian mystics understood union with the Divine in terms of *contemplatio*, a Latin word that Gregory the Great of the sixth century described as "the knowledge of God that is impregnated with love."[4]

The evidence shows that the pattern of *contemplation*—the preferred term for meditation in the Christian tradition—was established in Christ's own ministry. However, words like *gnosis* and *contemplatio* came later by way of theological reflection; they attempted to point to the reality of Christ being One with the Father (see John 10:30)—a reality that was synonymous with His capacity to atone. I want to make this theme of *atonement* a bit more explicit at this point in the book.

Traditionally in Christianity, the Atonement refers to Christ's necessary salvific act to redeem the world from its fallenness. According to Christian belief, only Christ in His divinity and perfection could effectively offer Himself on behalf of mankind.

And yet, core to Latter-day Saint theology is our own divinity, yours, and mine—including all of the human family. If Christ in His divine capacity was able to atone, can we not atone also in our own divinity? Eugene England wrote that atonement is "a bringing to unity, a reconciliation of that which is estranged: man and man, man and God, or man and himself."[5] This definition is consistent with William Tyndale's usage of *atonement* in the King James Bible and one of the earliest meanings of the word in the English language: "to be one with."[6]

Recall in chapter two that as we increase in being, as we wake up through each distinct center of Intelligence, our perception shifts, and we begin to directly experience our *being One with* all that is, even as Christ was One with the Father. Here in chapter three, I will trace out a similar path of "One-ing" by way of unifying the mind and keeping an eye single on the Glory of God. In any event, my argument throughout this book will be that the transformative process itself is in fact the path of "at-one-ment" that we are all given to walk as human beings. It is a path that Jesus modeled for us historically and one that is now available for us every moment in Divine Reality.

As we wake up and reconcile the different aspects of ourselves, we simultaneously reconcile ourselves with one another and learn to perceive our shared essence with God and all that is Sacred. Loving God and loving our neighbor are seen to be two sides of the same coin, and we accomplish this radical act of love by continuously practicing at-one-ment every moment of our lives. Returning to the subject at hand, contemplation has been the traditional approach in Christianity for learning to become One with the Divine—literally at-one-ing. It is a true act of dying to everything we are not for the sake of more fully participating in the risen life of Christ.

Contemplation flourished in Christianity until around the sixteenth century. For complex reasons that are beyond the scope of this book, this highly refined form of prayer came to be viewed with distrust.[7] I'll limit myself to saying that the disrepute of contemplation corresponds almost perfectly with the advent of the European Enlightenment, a movement where the mind's knowing—rational, linear, empirical—became dominant, and all other forms of knowing fell under suspicion. Since that time, the mode of prayer most Christians are familiar with today—discursive prayer, essentially talking to God—came to be viewed as the only available option. The promise of full union, atonement with the Divine through prayer practice, faded into obscurity as the thinking mind took center stage in prayer life.

What I want to stress is that when we talk about having an "eye single," we are in fact *restoring* something precious that has been lost. Meditation, the contemplative life, is not some New Age fad. It has been present and vital in Christ's gospel since the beginning. We

Christians who have come of age in the last few centuries are anomalous in our contemplative illiteracy, though we seldom realize it.

When I describe this history of contemplation and the historic practices used to develop concentration to Latter-day Saints, a question inevitably comes up: if concentration is so important, then why don't we teach it at church? There are a lot of ways to answer this. Perhaps thinking about the Restoration as a global phenomenon rather than something unfolding exclusively through The Church of Jesus Christ of Latter-day Saints is a good place to start.

If we zoom out and look at the planet as a whole, there's no question there is currently a global renaissance in concentration practices. Whether we look to the Christian contemplative revival or the mindfulness "revolution" sweeping the globe, human beings in the modern, digital world are keenly interested in training the mind in concentration. This global interest strikes me as deeply intuitive: in an age where we are more chronically distracted than any human beings to ever inhabit the planet, of course we'll need a countervailing force to keep our attention on what matters most. In this sense, meditation practices are all but the inevitable response to digital technologies that can potentially destabilize our mental and spiritual health. It is humanity as a whole then, not simply the Church, that is already well on its way to restoring contemplation to a more prominent role in spiritual life.

The movement I'm describing is imbalanced, though. Currently, the styles of meditation and concentration practices we're seeing in classrooms, healthcare systems, throughout society—they all have quite a strong Buddhist flavor. "Mindfulness," in fact, derives from ancient Buddhist practices.

The question I feel compelled to ask as a Latter-day Saint with a contemplative heart is this: How can we as a people and a Church *restore and evolve* our own style of contemplation, including unique insights from our tradition that would lead to the theosis of humanity?

In the book of Mosiah, we're commanded to "pray without ceasing, and to give thanks in all things" (26:39). This type of prayer requires some serious stamina! The call to contemplation, to live in a state of continuous prayer, is clear. If we're going to make this a reality, we need to train like the elite spiritual athletes our Divine Excellence asks us to be. I would argue that among the most basic fundamental skills on this path is concentration.

If we train our minds and our hearts to stay focused on the Glory of God, we will be filled with Light. We will come to comprehend all things and to know the very Mind and Heart of God. If we don't intentionally cultivate concentration, on the other hand, we will become distracted. Especially in today's world, with limitless opportunities to amuse ourselves, to numb out, we will figuratively *fall asleep* in the garden again and again as Christ prays in our midst. The untrained mind will be tossed about by the winds of distraction. In our modern times, distraction may be the most potent form of temptation.

FILLED WITH LIGHT

As we proceed, note that I use the word *Light* in the context of concentration. I do this because to me, it feels most native to Latter-day Saint theology. We see it repeated throughout the scriptures, including "whatsoever is light is Spirit" (Doctrine and Covenants 84:45) and "the Lord God giveth light unto the understanding" (2 Nephi 31:3). Light is Divine Intelligence. It is that which *knows* and that which *grows*. It is a Reality more immense than I can begin to name.

That said, I've found it helpful to understand that in contemporary spirituality, words like *awareness* and *consciousness* are often pointing at something similar to *Light*. *Consciousness* and *awareness* are more secular, even scientific, terms referring to the basic fact of being awake and sensitive to experience. *Light*, on the other hand, has a more religious connotation and points to the divine essence that we fundamentally are. Importantly, this divine essence, among other things, is fundamentally awake, or aware. That is why you'll see some overlap with both secular and religious terms: Light is fundamentally aware. Spirit is conscious. Some people even mix ancient and modern categories and use phrases like "conscious spirit" or "aware presence." In what follows, I will tend to use the word *Light* since I prefer its connotations of Sacred Reality, but I will also make use of the words *consciousness* and *awareness*. The context will make clear what I'm describing.

Also, it will be helpful here to offer some additional nuances regarding concentration itself. Typically, when we think of concentration, we associate it with a narrowing of attention, almost a laser-like focus on one aspect of experience while disregarding everything else for a duration of time. When I refer to concentration, I'm including both exclusive and inclusive qualities of awareness. For example, when you need to dig a small sliver out of your finger with a delicate pair of tweezers, you shine a bright light on the area if you can, squint your eyes a bit, and forget about the rest of the world for a moment. On the other hand, when you reach the summit of a mountain after a good day's hike, your awareness naturally opens up to take in the panoramic expanse. Both examples involve concentration, but one is *focused concentration* while the other is wide *open*. These qualities are significant in the context of our centers of Intelligence; in one moment, we might be hyperfocused on an insight taking shape in the mind, while in another moment, we may be more panoramically aware of a fullness of joy arising in body, heart, and mind simultaneously.

A further detail to bear in mind is that concentration practice very much corresponds to our beloved polarity of works and Grace. When we start on the path of concentration, it naturally feels effortful, like we're doing a lot of work. But over time, we learn to let go, yield to the Divine Will, and let the greater Light *meditate* us. It's as if, after all we can do, the Sacred gathers us up and anoints us in Its Blessing. (This is the style of concentration most closely associated with contemplation.) Effortful concentration creates the conditions for effortless Light to pour through our being. In essence, concentration is how we shape the Divine Light over which we're given agency.

Now that we're better equipped to explore the path of concentration, I want to revisit the verse I opened this chapter with: "And if your eye be single to my glory, your whole bodies shall be filled with light, and there shall be no darkness in you; and that body which is filled with light comprehendeth all things" (Doctrine and Covenants 88:67).

When we read scripture, my feeling is that some passages lend themselves readily to a poetic or metaphorical interpretation. I don't believe this verse is one of them. For me, this verse is actually pointing to a spiritual reality we can give ourselves to—a reality we can learn to *become*.

We hear about Buddhist mindfulness, a *calm abiding* in our natural state. Or mantra meditation in the Hindu tradition, which consists of repeating sacred syllables imbued with divine meaning and creative power. But I love the Latter-day Saint formulation of concentration in this verse: "if your eye be single to my glory, your whole bodies shall be filled with light." This is a bold statement, even a divine promise. If we learn to hold our gaze, our whole attention on God, we will be illuminated—our *gnosis* perfected.

When I share this scripture with Latter-day Saints who are interested in learning meditation, most of them, if not all, tend to understand this verse as a description of something that will eventually happen at some point in the distant future. The language of the scripture is so removed from our ordinary experience, we've learned to temper our expectations that something even remotely like it could ever happen as long as we're living this human life.

There is some truth to this perspective. None of us will be *fully* transfigured into pure Light and come to comprehend all things in our mortal state. And yet we have a scriptural account of when this happened to a human being on this very earth that we now walk. I would suggest that the language of an "eye single" from the Doctrine and Covenants points directly to the event on the Mount of Transfiguration. From my reading, it's a literal account of a body being translated into pure Light.

In the Doctrine and Covenants, we're given a simple set of practice instructions. We're told that if we can train our mind to be single to God's Glory as Christ did, this ability will catalyze a process whereby our own being is gradually transformed into pure Light. In a complementary scripture, it reads: "That which is of God is light; and he that receiveth light, and continueth in God, receiveth more light; and that light groweth brighter and brighter until the perfect day" (Doctrine and Covenants 50:24).

The basic sequence these scriptures reveal are as follows: develop the skill to keep an eye single to God's Glory. If you do this, Sacred Reality will pour Light into you until you are eventually nothing but Light. Being pure Light, you will be "perfect" and comprehend all things.

Again, the elemental skill at play here is concentration, and concentration can be cultivated. We happen to be living in a particular moment in Christianity where there is less appreciation for the role of concentration, for contemplation, than there has been in a very long time. Yet interest is resurgent. In my view, contemplation is a precious truth of Christ's gospel that waits to be fully restored. To whatever extent any of us sincerely practices maintaining an eye single to the Glory of God, we will experience the very process of transfiguration the scriptures bear witness to. Our own transfiguration will unfold differently than that of Jesus. But it will be a difference in degree, not in kind. A difference in quantity, not quality. It will unfold according to a timeline that is unique to us and the journey of our soul, but the end result will be the same. What manner of human being ought we to be? Even as Christ is (see 3 Nephi 27:27). We are born to comprehend more and more of Divine Reality until the perfect day.

THE ROLE OF PRACTICE

Though we're not accustomed to talking about high states of concentration and the intense spiritual energies that tend to flow from keeping our *eye single*, there's a story in the Latter-day Saint tradition that illustrates this all quite strikingly.

In 1832 at the Johnson Home in Hiram, Ohio, Philo Dibble witnessed Joseph Smith and Sidney Rigdon receive the vision of the degrees of glory (what later became Doctrine and Covenants 76). His eyewitness testimony makes for a textbook example of the fruits of a mature spiritual practice. Dibble, a bystander, reports: "I saw the glory and felt the power, but did not see the vision."[8] He goes on to mention a key comment from Joseph: "Joseph sat firmly and calmly all the time in the midst of a magnificent glory, but Sidney sat limp and pale, apparently as limber as a rag. Observing which, Joseph remarked, smilingly, 'Sidney is not used to it as I am.'"[9]

As I see it, there is an important clue in this text: Sydney slumps in his chair, pale and limp, while Joseph sits serene, radiating Light from within. He glances over and remarks in good humor, "Sidney is not used to it as I am." Joseph clearly understood that these high-energy spiritual states are something *we can get used to*. Absorption in Divine Glory isn't as much about a singular experience we attain somehow so much as a state of being we are continually invited into through inexhaustible Grace. In fact, it's been said in the contemplative

AN EYE SINGLE | 61

traditions that *meditation isn't something we learn to do, it's something we get used to.*

The sacred traditions of the world express significant agreement on this point—from the imaginal world spoken of in Islam to the Buddhist realms of power. There is tremendous spiritual energy, higher realities all about us, in us, and through us. But if we don't become used to these higher realities in our conscious experience, we will miss out on the joy of more fully embodying them. It is God's good pleasure to give us the kingdom. Every moment represents a precious opportunity to receive this unsurpassable gift with faith and wholeheartedness.

If we take up the practice of concentration, the practice of keeping an eye single to God's Glory, we can learn to remain open to these luminous realms. Our bodies, hearts, and minds, our very being, *gets used to* more and more Light. Little by little, we become more *willing* to accept the staggering Abundance and Generosity of the Sacred.

When we give ourselves to the inner path of transformation, stabilized with powerful concentration, the spiritual energy can become incredibly intense, like a magnifying glass burning a hole through a leaf. I remember times in my own contemplative practice where the sense of joy, the sense of Divine Love was so powerful, it felt as if my physical senses couldn't tolerate it. It was almost searingly painful to experience Divine Presence so concentrated, and yet I knew the pain was redemptive. The prophet Nephi in the Book of Mormon describes a related experience poetically: "My God…hath filled me with his love, even unto the consuming of my flesh" (2 Nephi 4:20–21).

When our eye is single and our will fully open, it can feel as if Divine Presence is incinerating our tissues and cells. It feels *as if* our very flesh is being consumed, at least at first. But as the Prophet Joseph suggests, we too can get used to the Flame that in fact does not consume. As we mature on the contemplative path, as our nervous systems grow accustomed to channeling more wattage, we realize that we're participating in a transfiguring process. We're being filled with Light in a way and at a rate that is completely unique and personal to us. God is pouring out as much blessing over us as we can possibly stand.

WORSHIP

As we work more deliberately with concentration as a spiritual practice, other crucial elements of the spiritual life come into sharper focus. Take worship, for example. When we use the word *worship*, we often mean the rites and rituals associated with religious life. We worship at a designated place and in a particular way. Worship might involve a number of things, like going to church, praying, or reading scriptures—all concrete acts of faith. But in the context of keeping an eye single to the Glory of God, *worship* takes on a more subtle, pervasive meaning. I propose that *worship is none other than what we consciously attend to, moment to moment, in our daily lives.* Whatever it is we pay attention to, we are implicitly worshiping.

For example, if we pay attention to our reputation and social standing, we're elevating and magnifying the importance of these things. If we pay attention to the belief that we need to make more money, we're actually making that belief an object of worship. In another moment in life, we might find ourselves paying special attention to the love we have for our child or the gratitude we feel for the planet earth that sustains our life. In yet another moment, we might be paying attention to a gnawing anger we feel towards a loved one who failed to understand our sincere intent. The point is, every act of attention represents what we value in that moment. Where our heart is, there will be our treasure. In contemporary terms, *attention always follows intention.*

This framing requires clarification. Lest we succumb to scrupulosity here, I want to be very clear that I am not suggesting we should *never* pay attention to money, reputation, or anything else. If anything, the values and intention underlying our attention are paramount. One person may focus on amassing more wealth as a poor substitute for cultivating a deeper relationship with God. Another person might focus on making more money to pay for the care of a sick child.

While we are never adequate to judge the quality of another person's worship, we can certainly begin to take a more conscious inventory of where our attention goes moment to moment each day. This is a humbling process. What we attend to, we assign value to. What we assign great value to, we end up adoring and worshiping.

Conscious awareness proves to be a powerful spiritual resource. If what we attend to naturally grows and flourishes, then the inverse is also true: what we don't pay attention to naturally contracts, diminishes, and falls into unconsciousness. One of the most significant examples of this principle in my own life has been my relationship with my parents.

For years, while I was traveling and living abroad, I felt an aversion to all things Utah, where I'd grown up. I visited as seldom as I could, and not fully realizing it at the time, I avoided contacting people from back home as well. When I traveled from Shanghai to attend my sister's wedding in my early thirties, I realized that my relationships with family members, with my parents especially, had atrophied. It didn't sit well with me. When I really felt the lack of attention I'd invested in these people that I truly loved, I decided right then and there that if I was in town, I was going to have Sunday dinner with them every week from that moment on. No exceptions. What followed was an eleven-year period full of hundreds of Sunday dinners and no shortage of disturbing moments for me.

Especially the first few years, heartache and memories I'd been avoiding most of my life would resurface in random moments—when I would reach for more homemade strawberry jam or sweep the floor after dinner. Or the pain would percolate up in less random moments, like when the dinner table discussion would turn towards my siblings' Church callings (I had been inactive in the Church for twenty years and didn't love that topic at first). Sometimes I'd leave the table and go sit in the bathroom just to take some deep breaths to help with the intense feelings coming up. But slowly, the intention to heal with my parents, to repair what had been damaged, took effect. During those years, which are among the most precious memories of my life now, I felt the healing Light of Christ transfigure our relationships. Genuine friendship and easy laughter slowly replaced any sense of alienation I once felt. The recipe? Time and loving attention. As Fritz Perls famously said, "Awareness *per se*—by and of itself, can be curative."[10]

To understand the power of conscious awareness in another way, think about when you're with somebody who pays complete attention to you. They are fully present with you and only you. You know by the quality of their presence and attention that you are valuable. You are important to this person.

I had a powerful experience with a business partner that transformed my understanding of presence. Years ago my colleague and I had routine calls throughout the week to discuss the business we were involved in together. Over time, I realized that at different points in our conversations he would say things like, "Hey, I'm getting into the car. Is it okay if we talk for the next fifteen minutes while I'm driving?" I didn't think too much of it at first. "Yeah, of course that's okay," I would respond, even though I was thinking to myself, "Why did he even mention that?"

After a few months of this, it began to dawn on me that every time my colleague's attention or presence was divided in any way, he made me aware of it. He never sat me down and said, "Hey, Thomas, I love you and I value you. That's why I'm telling you that I'm not able to be as present with you as I would like to be right now." But that *is* what his attention and his presence were communicating to me. My colleague had a strong intention to consecrate his attention to every moment of our relationship. As a result over time, I began to feel more holy when I was with him. He attended to me so deeply that I came to feel how *worthy* I was of someone's full attention. That's the power of presence. When we give ourselves fully to something, we implicitly say, "I value this. This is worthy of my life energy, of my spirit." I believe that being fully present is the *only* way God knows how to be with us. Each of us is holy to our Divine Parents.

In a spiritual sense, we become what we worship. If I have an intention every day to attend to God's all-pervasive Love, then everything I see, hear, and feel will become infused with more of God's Love over time. Just by remaining present to God's Love more often, I will invite more of that Love into my being.

Remember that I'm not suggesting a mechanical practice of keeping scrupulous inventory of where our attention goes every second. We don't need to think, "Right now, I'm paying attention to filing my income taxes before the deadline. Now I'm wondering whether the potato salad in the fridge has gone bad. Oh, no—I don't mean to worship the potato salad!" It's simpler and more graceful than that: we can sanctify each moment of life with our wholehearted awareness and engagement. To have an eye single to God's Glory is an act of consecration. It is how we sanctify each moment with the Light of our awareness.

LIFE PRACTICE: CONSECRATING YOUR ATTENTION

Notice in life when you're less than present with what's right in front of you. Once you notice, try and quantify how much of you is present and how much of you is elsewhere. Are you 50 percent present? 80 percent present? Once you notice you're divided, practice coming back to full presence. Feel the distinct pleasure of becoming 100 percent present again. Notice the sensory richness when you're fully present with whatever you choose to be present with.

Practice this exercise especially when you're present with other human beings. If you're not able to be 100 percent present, notice that. You might try telling the person you're with that you're a little bit distracted at the moment. Do this with the intention of letting others know how valuable their presence is to you and that you don't want to miss out on it. It doesn't matter if it's your best friend or the clerk at the grocery store—we all deserve one another's full presence!

CONCENTRATION AS TRUST

A meditation student of mine who practices therapy with horses said something years ago that struck me as both true and beautiful.

She explained to me that horses naturally like to keep one eye scanning the environment for danger, to be on the lookout for predators. With their other eye, they'll often engage you if you come up close to them and make contact. But when a horse squares off with you and focuses solely on you, what they're communicating in all their majesty is that they trust you entirely. In essence, the horse is completely undefended before you. "When a horse gives me both eyes," she said, "I feel completely honored."

This absolute trust is a beautiful image of concentration. We humans also tend to have at least one eye scanning the environment for danger or problems. Unlike the horse, though, our other eye is often scanning for entertainment, distraction, anything to whisk us away from the boredom and drudgery of the routines we feel stuck in.

Like the horse, we can give "both eyes" to whatever we choose. We can learn to give our entire being, undivided and undefended, to whatever it is we set our hearts upon. As we explored in the above section, whatever we value, we will tend to pay attention to and put our whole heart there, our whole being. We'll give it both eyes.

From a place of absolute trust, there are no worries left in the mind, no gnawing doubts. There is no longer any restlessness and no taking thought for the morrow. There's nothing we have to manage other than the giving of our whole self to the Divine in whom we have total confidence.

I remember an especially vivid experience I had in trusting the Divine completely. A long time ago now, I was spending the week with my Buddhist teacher at his monastery. We were meditating long hours with the intention of bringing the mind into a deep state of concentration. All at once, something within me stopped struggling, and I forgot myself entirely. What happened after that I can't say, because there was literally not a single reflection on the moment. I had disappeared into utter Simplicity. By some happy accident, I had unintentionally offered both eyes to the Mystery.

At some point, I snapped out of that profound state of concentration—that is, trust—and found myself sitting still in the meditation hall where I'd been all along. The world was now achingly alive, my senses crisp like crackling thunder. I felt like I'd just been born. And yet, nothing had happened. Literally, nothing. There was no trace of any special experience. No memory. I was just there. New.

Without a conscious thought, just a few days later, I found myself wandering into a chapel to take the sacrament and to remember Christ. I hadn't done so in nearly twenty years.

What meaning can I make of this experience? As a longtime meditator, I hadn't consciously been seeking to know Christ. But when I gave *both eyes* to Sacred Reality, when I let my defenses down and trusted, Christ took hold of my heart and claimed me as His own Body and Spirit. Walking back into a sacrament meeting is where my experience led me. I wonder where yours will lead you.

UNIFYING THE MIND

When we take up the practice of maintaining an eye single to the Glory of God, we face challenges. To experience this for yourself, I invite you to go somewhere secluded and focus on the Divine for an entire hour. Or eight hours if you're feeling confident. Whatever the amount of time, tell yourself, "I'm not going to move, I'm not going to eat, I'm not going to drink, not going to check my texts or emails. I'm just going to be fully available to Divine Presence." You might notice that seconds later, your mind is wandering off in a thousand different directions that have nothing to do with your original intention. Why is this? Why won't the mind stay when we ask it to stay?

This is a question we need to stop on and consider deeply. If we're not honest about the challenges we're up against, we'll likely live in denial that these challenges really do exist. If we pretend that chronic mind-wandering and distractedness aren't our baseline state, we will pay lip service to keeping an eye single to God's Glory while our attention is continually scattered. If we don't acknowledge the difficulty of training a fragmented mind, the potency of our transformation will remain limited.

Let me put it in more stark terms. If the state of our everyday mind is one of chronic distractedness and a predisposition to focus on, even obsess over, problems and negative mind states, how much choice do we really have in life? Mind training is profoundly humbling because it reveals, with increasing clarity, how much of the time we're not in choice, not free to choose at all. In the restored gospel, I think we rightly emphasize the importance of agency above other virtues. What we don't pay enough attention to is the *spectrum of agency* we all occupy. That is, when our eye is single, our mind unified, we can intentionally respond to life with greater choice. However, in other moments, when we're fragmented and bent on avoiding our own discomfort, we act compulsively, with little choice at all.

We often speak of drug addicts as a different class of people with a very visible problem different from our own. We imagine they're like prisoners to insatiable cravings, desperate to escape from their cells. A closer look at what motivates us all at a very deep level reveals that we too are desperate to avoid certain feelings. We're often looking for a "hit" of any kind for momentary relief from our suffering. We are addicts pretending that we're free to shop or free to check our social media for the twentieth time in one hour. In the context of concentration practice and worship, few of us have as much choice in directing our moment to moment attention as we would like.

Modern neuroscience paints a vivid image of what's occurring in our wandering minds. Prior to recent discoveries, there was a tendency to think about ourselves as a single entity: I am an individual, a free moral agent. And as an agent, I can assert my will to do what I want to do in the world. This understanding of ourselves is useful to an extent. But if we look closer at the mind's workings, the story that neuroscience unfolds has a great deal to offer our current understanding of agency. Ultimately, it speaks to how we choose to receive more or less Light in our lives.

The current scientific understanding of the mind is that it's not just a uniform whole constituted by a single purpose at a given time. The mind is actually better understood as a complex network of innumerable processes, "subminds," most of which are unconscious, all pulling in different directions with their conflicting intentions.

What we understand to be "executive functioning" in the brain includes an inhibiting function that is capable of overriding the automatic impulses that often get the best of us. In religious terms, executive functioning in the brain is something like our "higher self" that is capable of overriding the urges of the natural man and woman. From this higher seat of consciousness, we can judge the relative value of all the competing intentions that are present *within us* at a given time. At a certain point, we make a conscious decision and take a course of action.[11] The following example will clarify this concept.

Say I'm lounging around the house, feeling a little bored, and suddenly have a craving for a milkshake. The image, taste, and smell of the milkshake suddenly take form in my mind's eye. Instantly my body responds to the mental image and starts to mobilize energy towards procuring this creamy cache of calories. Then all at once, my reverie is interrupted when I spontaneously remember how awful I felt the last time I indulged this urge: brain fog and indigestion that lasted well into the night. The tables have turned, and what now looms large in conscious awareness are the negative feelings associated with eating too much dairy. Other subconscious processes of the mind are exposed to this information and integrate it into their own "decision-making processes" that are happening far beneath the threshold of my conscious awareness. Some part of "me," some aspect of the mind, is still craving the milkshake. Another part of "me" is asserting its will and agenda to protect "me" from the milkshake. I put "me" in quotation marks because so far, this process is playing out through various subminds, and "I" haven't consciously participated in any of it yet. I'm at the whim of the many parts that constitute what I call "me." What is this poor creature of appetite to do? At what point does agency become involved?

The key lies in learning to hold a strong, *conscious intention* in awareness over sustained periods of time. Without conscious intention, our unconscious intentions all attempt to take control of the cockpit and navigate us toward their destination of choice—whatever the consequences. Whether our intentions are conscious or not, from a neuroscientific view, there are often many competing intentions in the mind-system at a given time. And *attention always follows intention*.

When we hold a strong, conscious intention, the different parts of the mind pulling in different directions gradually start to unify and move in one *conscious* direction. Essentially, this practice is the neuroscientific description of training our "eye," or "I," to be single. This process, though effortful at first, pays enormous dividends over time. When conscious intention is maintained and directed toward what we value most, the rest of the subminds start to get with the program. Our animal impulses that prefer to indulge their appetites get a taste of the conscious intention to receive Divine Light, and they like it. Through a trickle-down effect, the parts of us that are most compulsive and resistant to change—we would say *sinful* in a theological context—are transformed by the one and only thing that can truly nourish us. In the end, we have the experience of being more choiceful because each different aspect of ourselves has tasted true conversion and freely chooses "the right." That is, the subminds are willing to give up immediate gratification for what they wanted all along anyway. In a manner of speaking, what we all long for is an increased measure of Divine Life, Love, and Light.

Rarely in life are we so aligned with ourselves that all of the subprocesses and aspects of self are moving in the same direction. More often, the different aspects of ourselves are like a team of oxen yoked to a large ring at the center, all pulling in different directions. In these moments, we exert great effort and get exactly nowhere. Or in Paul's words, "I love to do God's will so far as my new nature is concerned; but there is something else deep within me, in my lower nature, that is at war with my mind and wins the fight and makes me a slave to the sin that is still within me" (Romans 7:22–23[12]). Joining ancient and modern expressions, our *lower nature* represents unconscious intentions to pursue impulses and desires that cannot bring us the happiness we seek. *New nature* represents consciously held intention coming from the "higher self." This is the part of us that loves to align itself with Holy Will.

States of a unified mind do arise spontaneously from time to time in life. When we're engaged in our profession or area of expertise, we often experience a quality of absorption. Sometimes when we're playing our favorite sport, we enter a flow state. It can happen in nature—the dancing vitality of Life itself vibrates within our very cells, and our boundaries begin to blur with the wild. It can happen in an intimate encounter with our partner or when we're lost in the good company of a friend we haven't seen in a long time.

Each of us drop into these unified states from time to time by Grace. But most of the time, we're fragmented. What if we didn't have to be engaged in our favorite activity in order to feel such peace and pleasure? It's my experience that most people don't want to just accidentally fall into a unified state; they want to go there and remain at will. Both revealed scripture and modern science tell us that we can do the work that allows for this Grace. We can train our minds to have an eye single so that experiences with Divine Presence no longer feel like random accidents but conscious co-creation with God. As we do so, we're filled with more of the Light that would transform us into new creatures.

FALL BEHIND THE DISPLAY

I mentioned the role of solitude in contemplative life earlier. In Luke 5:16, we read that Jesus "often withdrew to lonely places and prayed" (NIV). If even Jesus sought solitude during his earthly mission, how much more so do we need solitude to fortify our prayer life in an age of hyperstimulation? Left to our own devices, we are almost constantly feeding on the content of the mind. Add to that already bloated diet a feed of information through our digital devices, and we've got a bona fide case of sensory gluttony. Solitude—a practice of *sensory fasting*—is a prerequisite to concentration practice that we need now more than ever.

Solitude works on a literal and a more subtle level. Literally, it really is helpful when training the mind to find a quiet space, even if it's only a few minutes a day away from all the major commotion. At a more subtle level, though, solitude is the quality of remaining wholly given to the Sacred throughout the day, regardless of circumstance. If we don't learn to wake from the constant daydream we're in, we'll be lulled continually by the mind's productions and sleepwalk our way through life. Remember that to feel Divine Presence is to be *awake*—embodied at all levels at once.

My wife and I have a dog and are endlessly amused by her obsession with squirrels. If she sees a squirrel, if she even hears us say the word *squirrel*, everything in her world stops, her attention completely captured by her quarry. We all have dog consciousness in this way. Deep down, we know what matters most to us, but the moment we hear "squirrel," the moment we see a shiny object flash before us, we're off to the races. We sell our birthright for a mess of pottage a thousand times a day. We tell ourselves, "I want to be more prayerful. I want to enter God's rest." Then out of nowhere a thought intrudes, "Any emails come in the last twenty minutes?" Or, "I feel bored—I'll text a friend." Or, we had a fight with our friend and we can't stop turning it over in our minds and rehearsing our story of persecution. We get glued to channel "me" and can't pry ourselves away from the drama. We need to learn to fall back, to fall behind the intoxicating display of experience. In doing so, we come to remember a Rest that is deeper than the body knows, deeper than the mind can comprehend.

In the previous chapter, I described the different levels of embodiment that are available to all of us. In restored gospel theology, we can think about these as increasingly pure and refined levels of matter—Holy all the way up and down (see Doctrine and Covenants 131:7–8). We can be physically embodied, energetically embodied, mentally, emotionally, and even spiritually embodied. By spiritually embodied, I mean we can even learn to rest in a place of pure Intelligence, or open awareness. Here we're primarily aware of the simple feeling of Being itself. This awareness is very much a capacity we can cultivate in this human estate. However, without conscious intention, we end up not developing this vital skill. We end up not systematically training our capacity to be truly embodied. Once in a while, we might slip into a Grace-filled experience—spontaneously freed from all the mental-emotional clutter that typically dogs us. There are moments we do fall behind the display and taste brief joy. These experiences are so different in quality from all the other dull moments that fill our lives that we say to ourselves, "Wow, that was *incredible*. For a moment there I felt like I was connected to everything. Like I'd come home. How do I get back there?" Coming home does not have to be an accident. We have the spiritual capacity to fall behind the display of the mind's contents again and again until we find our center of gravity in a new self that is centered in Christ's Divine Life. Christian contemplatives have called this our "true self." Its nature is joy, freedom, and Infinite Love.

To find this new center of gravity, we need to first withdraw. We need to withdraw as Jesus did, to lonely places, into solitude, if only for just a few minutes at first. Over time as we find a new equilibrium in stillness, it's not even about physically withdrawing. The practice becomes the subtle skill of paying attention in a new way and from a new place in ourselves. We learn at will to fall behind the cacophony of noise, the frenetic energy of the thinking mind, and the turbulent emotions of the heart. Through Grace and works, we learn to keep one foot planted in the deep abiding peace and Presence of God—in our true self—no matter what the conditions are around us.

RESTING IN STILLNESS

The language "search, ponder, and pray" points to powerful fundamentals in spiritual life. I've added to this tried and true formula an element that is already implicit: stillness (see Psalms 46:10: "Be still, and know that I am God."). We can establish ourselves in stillness, then search, ponder, pray, and *rest*, in any order that feels intuitive.

When we search, ponder, and pray, we generally emphasize *doing*. They are activities. Rest and stillness, on the other hand, imply *being*. They emphasize the absence of activity. As one translation of the *Tao Te Ching* reads, "Keep sharpening your knife and it will blunt."[13] Ironically, searching for answers in the mind too persistently blunts our spiritual acuity. When the mind is overly reliant on the same patterns of thinking, it becomes dull. However, when we rest in the simple feeling of Divine Being, we become as a child again—supple, humble, open to possibility.

One of my favorite "styles" of prayer is to spend a good amount of time—thirty minutes or more if the toddler is sleeping!—just settling. I sit still and let body, heart, and mind become clear like a pond whose silt has settled all the way to the bottom. I wait until the stillness is so thick I could kiss it, then I look *from* the heart. I form an intention to say something real to God, whatever it is. Often, it is just a few words that rise up from the dark waters. "God, help me remember You today."

The words come from such a deep place, deeper than "me," that even as they take shape in my mind, I feel them changing me, infusing me with energy. That's a telltale sign that something deeper is praying through us—we feel surprised and deeply affected by the words taking shape in the field in which we live and move and have our being (see Acts 17:28).

As an experiment, you can practice resting in silence and noticing how long you can tolerate being utterly quiet before the mind conjures up a thought or a distraction. For most of us, just a few seconds of silence starts to feel intolerable. The body gets restless, the mind agitated or even painfully bored. We need to train ourselves to rest deeply in the silence, to join ourselves *with* the silence. When we make a home of silence, we begin to realize that this silence—the dazzling dark—is profoundly *fertile*. It is spiritually alive and active. We experience the paradox that utter stillness in the Sacred is teeming with Creativity, Love, Insight, and Power.

In other words, when we train ourselves to rest in stillness, we become more sensitive to the revelation and the inspiration that arises out of the Sacred Stillness itself. At that point, with an eye single to God's Glory, searching, pondering, praying, and resting are all different expressions of one Divine Reality. It doesn't matter which direction we move in because every direction is Holiness. But if our point of departure lacks stillness, we run the risk of endlessly searching, thinking stale thoughts, talking *at* God, never pausing to listen from the generative Silence where our being and God's Being coincide.

To learn to rest in stillness, we need to start somewhere. Most of us can't just read a book like this one and say, "This meditation guy says we should sit still and rest in the Sacred. I like it. I'll do just that starting tomorrow morning." We already discussed that the brain is not amenable to that kind of training. We can have the best intention, the strongest resolution in the world to be in stillness and to not entertain a single distracting thought. We vow to drink in Divine Presence and worship God with all of our heart, mind, and soul. But five seconds later, we're going to see a squirrel and break that vow.

There's no need to fret, though. "By small and simple things are great things brought to pass" (Alma 37:6). Like an athlete training for a competition, we just need to introduce a touch of discipline into our discipleship. The words *discipline* and *disciple* share a common root for a reason. A little diligence and sincere intent go a long way in Sacred Reality. Hold a steady, conscious intention and get those reps in. As we do this, we become more used to this way of being human in the world. In practice, we need to develop the muscle memory of withdrawing from the vivid, intoxicating display of the mind. We need to develop a tolerance for stillness and the intense spiritual energy that comes pouring through just when we're ready to receive more of it.

INTRODUCTION TO REMEMBRANCE

MEDITATION
Remembrance

LIGHT KNOWS THE MIND

I'll conclude the chapter with another scripture that I love for its rich contemplative overtones. I come back to it again and again because I believe in a very succinct way, it points us back to our true identity in Christ: "And the light which shineth, which giveth you light, is through him who enlighteneth your eyes, which is the same light that quickeneth your understandings" (Doctrine and Covenants 88:11).

Conventionally, we think we are an individual seeking, maybe even striving, to know God. But this scripture says something more subtle, something we can easily look right past if we're not paying close attention. It is the Sacred Light Itself that "quickeneth" our understanding. It is not we, a self supposedly separate from God, that knows things with our mind. Rather, we, by way of Divine Light, know our own thinking. The Light, in other words, is *already* the very *substance* of our understanding. This is extraordinary.

Recall from chapter two the different ways of knowing that we explored—body, heart, and mind. But what is it that knows *through* the body? *Through* the heart and *through* the mind? According to Doctrine and Covenants 88, it is Light that knows through the body and Light that enlightens the heart. It is Light that knows the mind. From a Latter-day Saint perspective, we could say that pure Intelligence, or Spirit, *takes the shape* of the body, heart, and mind's knowing. Body, heart, and mind are the classical modes of knowing, but Intelligence, or Light, is the very substance of all these human faculties.

We—some self that is seemingly estranged from Sacred Reality—don't feel an emotion. It is Light that is aware of feeling. When we hear a sound, what is it that hears? Light is the Intelligence by which the ear hears. Divine Light is already that which experiences every experience we could possibly have in Sacred Reality. It is Divine Light that discerns the meaning of the words on this very page.

Our shame-driven striving can end right here. As we pay attention to this Light, as we pay attention *from* this Light, we learn to relax into our divine essence. This movement, I believe, is what Christ meant by *repentance*. We come to remember who we are at the deepest level. We take heart that Divine Reality is awakening through our bodies as Life, through our hearts as Love, and through our minds as Light, even now.

We have a choice to participate in this process. As we unify the mind, as we learn to keep an eye single on the only Reality that is worthy of our devotion, we learn to pray always and to become something entirely new.

INTRODUCTION TO OPEN-FOCUS

MEDITATION

Open-Focus

Chapter 4

The Sacred Heart

THE DANCING WALLS OF THE CHAPEL

One Sunday morning, I felt an almost alien impulse to put on a shirt and tie and walk down the street to my local Latter-day Saint meetinghouse. I hadn't attended Church meetings regularly since I was thirteen years old—nearly a twenty-year absence. In the interim, I had lived for extended periods in Asia, Europe, and many places in between.

If you'd asked me back then if I was happy, I could have looked you in the eye without hesitating and answered, "I'm happier than I dreamt I ever could be." You can think of me at that time as a well-adjusted, culturally Mormon, American Buddhist. My spiritual life had great momentum, consisting of meditation, sutra study, a strong intention to link my livelihood to the relieving of suffering, and meaningful relationships where I felt both seen and celebrated.

The point I want to make clear is that it's not as though I was in any kind of crisis. I was not looking for Jesus or religion. Though crisis can be a beautiful reason to examine faith more deeply, I had very little sense at that time that anything was missing for me personally.

And yet, there I was walking to church on a cool, clear Sunday morning in Salt Lake City. The first thing I noticed when I walked in the chapel was a beautiful, wall-size mural of the young Joseph Smith kneeling humbly on the Hill Cumorah, receiving gold plates from the angel Moroni. I was struck by what an unusual and beautiful piece of art it was to be hanging in a meetinghouse.

Nevertheless, I noticed as I scanned the room for an empty pew that my body was starting to get anxious for no apparent reason. At that point, I was having what I think a doctor would classify as a mild panic attack. The sense of threat began to build. My heart started to race noticeably, and I felt my throat constricting. The residue of unresolved emotional pain deposited so long ago in my organs, tissues, and cells was releasing back into my bloodstream. I felt just like I did when I was thirteen years old—the merciless inner critic jeered at me saying that everything I thought, felt, and did was awkward and *ugly*. My body itself felt like a cheap, ill-tailored suit that wouldn't sit properly on my frame no matter how much I wriggled and shifted.

In my distress I managed to find a seat off to the side. I sat waiting for the sacrament meeting to start, the blare of the organ piquing my sense of despair. The inner critic, that old familiar bully, began to interrogate me more harshly: "What were you thinking coming to church? You don't belong here." Growing up, especially by the time I was twelve years old or so, church had come to feel like all the suffering of my life distilled into a torturous three-hour block. That old poison was now percolating up from the depths. "Why am I here? I *hate* how I feel when I'm here."

Somewhere in my post-traumatic response to the old smell of hymnals, without any conscious effort, *something shifted*. I found a sense of spaciousness I'd learned to access through many years of Buddhist meditation. There was still a cacophony of thoughts in my mind and a distinct flavor of panic in my body. But I no longer *was* that panic. I was bigger than the panic, bigger than the voice of the critic, bigger than the whole chapel now.

My heart began to detect a loving Presence that just moments before had been blotted out by the squall in my body-mind. Whereas the thoughts and emotions whirling around felt like old pain rehashed, the Field of Light and Love I was sensing through my heart was like a gentle sunrise. The Presence felt old—the Ancient of Days—even as it was fresh and new in this moment. I looked around and marveled. The chapel, the music, the words, the souls gathered—they all felt so *alive*. The air itself seemed to sparkle. Though it might sound crazy to you, I swear the brick walls of that chapel were dancing in worship right along with us.

I think of my peers, I think of the upcoming generations of human beings who feel religion is a foreign, even benighted, mode of expression. For many, this perspective is often the thinking mind's appraisal of religious experience nowadays. But we know things through the heart that we can't know any other way. In fact, when we try to know something by the mind alone, we are often misled.

For me, my first visit back to Church after so many seasons away was a master class in the heart's way of knowing. By Grace, the heart's knowing prevailed that day. I felt the touch of an immense Love and Power that had been with me all along. I just didn't always have the eyes to see. I felt deeply and I knew clearly that there was genuine spiritual nourishment to be found within these walls. Here was a spring of water welling up to eternal life (see John 4:13).

DID NOT OUR HEARTS BURN WITHIN US?

My unexpected return to Church echoes what I take to be a central theme in the gospel: if our hearts are not awake and receptive, our ideas about who Christ is will prevent us from seeing Him.[1] For me, the story of the two disciples on the road to Emmaus (see Luke 24:13–35) is one of the most touching scriptural accounts of the heart's knowing.

In the story, two disciples are leaving Jerusalem and, we can imagine, are feeling utterly dejected. The one they had hailed as the Messiah, the one who was to redeem Israel and turn the tide of history, had been slain. Grief-stricken, they consoled one another on the dusty road home.

Another wanderer joins them along the way and essentially says, "Hey, what are y'all talking about? Why the long faces?" They seem incredulous that someone could have failed to hear about the calamity, as if to say, "Have you been living in a cave? Are you the only person in Jerusalem that hasn't heard the awful news?" They all get into a conversation, and the newcomer begins to point out in the scriptures, step by step, what is actually unfolding in real time. In their minds, Jesus had already been dead three days, proving that he was not the Son of God after all. But already their hearts were open to a more subtle reality.

As the day grew late, they encouraged the lone traveler to come home with them and rest. The stranger complied, broke bread with them at their table, gave thanks, and offered it to them. Then all at once, the very moment that the stranger offered them this sacrament, they suddenly saw Him—the Christ revealed in a flash of recognition. Then He disappeared.

What strikes me about this account is that as the two disciples grope to make sense of what had just happened, they have a sudden insight. Their words are some of my favorite in all of scripture: "And they said one to another, Did not our heart burn within us, while he talked with us by the way, and while he opened to us the scriptures?" (Luke 24:32, KJV).

The meaning that is most poignant for me in this verse is the mysterious way the heart knows what can't be known in any other way. When we're confused, struggling to make sense of unexpected events, it is the heart that intuits the entire resonant Field at once, announcing our place "in the family of things."[2] It is the heart that harmonizes with the song of redeeming Love. How do we know Christ? Do our hearts not burn within us?

The mind is keen. We use it to make fine distinctions, to detect patterns, to hone and refine the intuitions and insights that well up from the depths of consciousness. But without the support of the heart, the mind will turn in on itself in a closed system, its artifacts becoming rigid and brittle. Without the holistic knowing of the heart, which comprehends the holographic unity of the entire Field at once, we risk our ideas about God becoming empty symbols, even idols, disconnected from their *living* Source.

The heart is an exquisitely sensitive organ of perception, continually revealing to us the livingness of Christ in and through all things and our intimate participation with all of Divine Reality.

THE SUBTLE HEART

I've been using the word *heart* up until now and assuming that you understand what I mean. In fact, there are subtleties to this word and different experiential dimensions of the heart that I'd now like to make more explicit.

In an everyday context, when we say "heart," it means the living, beating organ in our chest. When I use the word *heart*, I am also talking about its physical nature. But the heart is so much more.

A metaphor I like to use to describe the heart's more subtle capacities is that of an antenna. An antenna is a piece of hardware that captures and transmits electromagnetic waves. These waves are forms of energy, information, and Intelligence all at once. Without the antenna, the information isn't meaningful. There's nothing to receive it, let alone to interpret and act on it. But if the antenna is functioning properly, it connects the listener to a veritable sea of communications.

Such is the heart. The heart has the capacity to attune to the great beyond, to register and receive information from the sea of Spirit in which we're immersed. As we make use of the heart in this way, treating it as the vital center of Intelligence that it is, we see our capacity for intuition, wisdom, and inspired action increase dramatically. We realize that signals of Divine Light often show up most powerfully in the physical, sensate organ of the heart only then to be interpreted and studied out in the mind.

In an even more subtle sense, the spiritual heart, or *Sacred Heart*, is seamlessly one with God and Divine Reality Itself. Here the metaphor of antenna breaks down. Whereas an antenna is made of metal that picks up on electromagnetic waves, I have come to see that the heart, at its most subtle level, is constituted of Divine Love Itself. It receives Divine Love and expresses Divine Love in one simultaneous act. The subtle heart is not ultimately separate from the Love, Light, and Intelligence with which it communicates. That is, it is not a separate *thing* perceiving other things. It is Love engendering Love; it is Light that knows Light.

The heart knows by joining with, by *becoming* what it knows (at-one-ing). It sympathetically resonates in such a way that there is no felt distance between the knowing heart and so-called object of perception. The subject-object distinction—characteristic of the mind's knowing—collapses into a taste of Union, or unitive knowing.

By extension, yet another way to understand the meaning of *heart* is as an individualized expression of the unitive Field of the

Divine. That is, the heart represents both our unique personhood as well as our absolute Oneness with the Divine all at once.[3] In Latter-day Saint terms, it is the local Intelligence of the unique self that is responsive to and resonant with the universal Light that is in and through all things (see Doctrine and Covenants 88:11–13).

To exercise the heart's knowing, we rely on the foundational skill of keeping an eye single. That is, concentration helps us stabilize our view *from* the heart. Notice the word *from*. In a mental-egoic culture, our first impulse is to observe the heart from the vantage point of the thinking mind. But as the heart's knowing gains momentum, we feel our center of gravity shift altogether. Rather than looking at the heart from thought, we learn to see with new eyes from the heart. We learn to feel and sense from the heart in a sustained way that gives rise to an entirely new sense of identity. As we wake up through the heart, we realize in a direct and awe-inspiring way that, like Divinity itself, we have no beginning or end.

EMBRACING JOY *AND* SORROW

To take up an abiding residence in the Sacred Heart and feel our at-one-ment with everything sounds like a sweet deal. So why aren't we all jumping at the opportunity? In part, it's because of pain.

Let's be honest: Life, in the best of circumstances, is significantly painful. The pleasures we seek often don't last as long as we'd like—for example, a relationship dissolves or our financial fortunes turn. Meanwhile, the most difficult experiences often last much longer than we'd prefer, whether it's a bout of physical illness, a season of faith crisis, or the ongoing suffering of our child. Even if we live a relatively pleasure-filled life, in the end, we're all asked to give up everything we've ever loved in this life at the moment of our death.

Because life is already painful by design, it's a counter-instinctual move to open up to even more pain, discomfort, and suffering. But this is exactly what the way of the heart asks of us. We start with a willingness to open up to more of our own pain. Then as we mature, we intuitively bring our presence and healing awareness to the pain of others.

When we undertake a heart practice in earnest, eventually we find that the Sacred Heart literally contains all things, excluding nothing. I look at Christ as the great archetype of this path. When He prays in Gethsemane, it is all of the pain, all of the sin, all of the sorrow of the entire world that He opens Himself up to. Feeling "good" was clearly not His highest priority on that dark night. As His disciples, our intention is to eventually feel everything, to help bear the burden of this everything with Christ in an infinite atonement. From this perspective, the atonement becomes an ongoing activity that we engage with Christ—something we all do for each other—rather than something Christ simply did for us. In the Gospel of Thomas, it reads:

> If you are searching,
> You must not stop
> until you find.
> When you find, however,
> You will become troubled.[4]

And there it is—written plainly on the page and conveniently omitted from the canon. If you see this practice through, at some point, you will be deeply disturbed. *You will become troubled.*

This path is markedly different from the mindfulness that is touted in today's popular spiritual culture—what I would call a "mindfulness lite." In mindfulness lite, the goal is primarily to feel good. If we're stressed, we reduce our stress by following simple breathing exercises. When we feel low, we meditate on objects of gratitude until we feel happy. To be sure, reducing stress and increasing gratitude are not bad things. We all need to feel good enough in a psychological sense in order to thrive. But as we mature spiritually, we need to mature beyond the need to always feel good. Just as God causes the sun to rise on the evil and the good alike, we learn in the way of the heart to bring caring awareness to life's joys as well as life's sorrows. A mature heart practice, then, is not about always trying to feel good. It is about being willing to feel *more*.

It is no coincidence that Christ was known as a man of sorrows. How could He not be with all the pain that His heart was awake to? And yet we also know through accounts in scripture that He was a man of transcendent joy—He was at-one with the Father and received everything the Father had. We're left with a paradox. The most joyful human being ever to walk the earth was supremely vulnerable to sorrow. In His joy, He was willing to descend to the depths of human misery, to give up His own life, and to plunge to the heart of the earth.

If we're going to work from the heart, this is the difficult path before us. Yes, unimaginable Love and Joy lie ahead, but so does dark, suffocating desolation that brings the strongest and most faithful to their knees. The Grace in this is that we're never asked to do more than we can do. We can only encounter so much of our own darkness and that of others at once. Fortunately, Sacred Reality has the patience of centuries and eons. We're given time to learn to dwell in the Fullness of Eternity.

I remember a period in my meditation practice that lasted many years. The Divine was slowly breaking my preferences down in a way I didn't yet have the maturity to discern. At the time, my basic understanding of a "good" meditation session was one where I experienced a pleasurable, sustained meditative state. If my mind got really quiet, that was good, I thought. If my heart felt full of love, also good. And I loved when I didn't feel physical pain during the meditation. Once in a while, the experience of my solid body thinned out into an energetic field—tingling, vibrating, alive, and flowing. The moment the experience ended, I would get anxious and wonder when the day would come that I could stay in that elevated state forever.

It took me a long time to really appreciate that Divine Reality was blessing me with both consolation *and* desolation all along the way. The consolation was exactly as I described above—God anointing me with a soothing Presence to encourage me, even heal my wounds. The desolation was a more fierce Grace that came in the form of God's absence. In that harrowing void, I was left to feel all the things I tried so hard to avoid feeling in daily life. My mind would thrash like a caged animal, my heart would cave in on itself, as if to say in a whimpering tone, "I will never be loved." Being exposed to the intensity of my own wounding thousands of times over taught me gradually that *something deeper in me* was strong enough to feel the things the surface "me" preferred not to feel. The desolation was pointing the way to how big my heart truly was and all that it could hold.

The process of waking up and sensitizing the heart can be like a painful thawing. When you go sledding or hiking in the winter and you've been out for hours, your fingers get freezing cold and grow numb. If they're numb enough, you can't move them very well. It's not painful—they're numb after all. But you've lost function. Then, you come back in by the hearth, warm your bones by the fire, and blood starts to flow back into your extremities. There's a moment when it's actually quite painful to regain sensation in your fingers and toes. Throbbing, stabbing, shooting pains beam through the nerves of the hands as your digits come back to life. Because we've been through this before, we don't panic. We know that too much numbness in the fingers for too long leads to frostbite and far more serious problems. So we welcome the temporary pain that means we're recovering function. It may be painful, but it's a good pain.

The work in the heart is similar. As human beings, too often we've become accustomed to living with a frozen heart. Like these numb fingers, the heart loses so much feeling, so much of its sensitivity.

In its hibernating state, the heart is not feeling, not resonating with the cries of joy and sorrow throughout time and space. It is no longer responding tenderly to the world.

Spiritually speaking, we need to undergo this thawing process. The heart can and must thaw to regain its proper function. The heart of stone becomes a *heart of flesh*. It's often painful. But it's a pain that signifies a recovering of function that we're meant to have, that we're born with—a function that is our birthright as children of noble descent. This function to be at-one with everything and to abide knowingly in the Sacred Heart is vital to our eternal progression and happiness.

NOISE AND SIGNAL

If avoiding pain is a major stumbling block in learning to live a more abundant life from the heart, then another challenge we face is sheer noise. To return to the metaphor of the antenna, the heart is an advanced spiritual instrument capable of harmonizing with signals across the entire spectrum of Intelligence. But alas, we are still human. Oftentimes the refined spiritual information that the subtle heart is so good at receiving gets drowned out by competing noise. In the previous chapter, we looked at the commotion of the fragmented mind in some detail and explored what it meant to train our eye to be single. Here in the territory of the heart, a similar challenge exists, only instead of divergent thoughts, it is the noise of intense emotion we must learn to filter out.

The heart's noisiness, or impurities, were well understood by the desert fathers and mothers. These were early Christian contemplatives (starting in the late third century) who sought solitude in harsh landscapes and practiced singular devotion to Christ. Through intensive prayer life, they came to be experts at the inner path and the various obstacles along the way to giving one's whole self over to the Divine—the way of at-one-ment.

The desert fathers and mothers used the word *passion* as a technical term that essentially points to any activity in the heart that fragments it and therefore interferes with our spiritual capacity to resonate with the Divine. Originally the term *passion* comes down to us from the Latin *patior*, which literally means "to suffer." But we need to do even a little more decoding here. The word *suffer* in archaic English, originally used to translate *passion* from Latin, emphasized "being acted upon."[5] The essence of the passions, then, are a loss of agency. The passions grip us. They hold us in their thrall. They are like mental-emotional grooves along which our energy and awareness are squeezed into a turbulent flow. Unless, that is, we consciously, intentionally create new pathways.

To purify the heart, we need to practice noticing the very moment the passions seize our faculties. When we're involuntarily gripped by an intense emotion—anger, jealousy, fear, pride—we learn we can let the disturbance pass without getting snared in the drama. Metaphorically, we start spotting these logjams on the river before they clog up the flow of energy. We let the current sweep the flotsam and jetsam downstream before we find ourselves tangled up in the debris.

This morning before writing, I took my dog and daughter for a walk around the neighborhood. In some moments, the rustle of the trees in the cool air, the silvery rays of the sun delighted me. My dog sniffing every last bush and telephone pole within his nose's reach was endlessly amusing. In other moments, I noticed powerful currents of feeling flowing through my heart. When I relaxed and let my awareness be open, the feelings coursing through me ranged from intense vulnerability, to grief, to love, to consolation. It all flowed like a powerful river with no discernible borders between the white water churning in the center and the more subtle eddies and slow currents flowing on the side. But the moment a judgmental thought took root—"this is all *his* fault"—the vast feelingness of the heart took on a tone of misery. The moment I allowed an ego-centered identity to interfere with the powerful forces of the heart, I felt my energy contract into a painful quality of anger. Energy would divert up to the thinking mind, taking the shape of familiar stories of feeling blamed and wronged by someone I love who I've been in conflict with. Those thoughts in turn would energize more emotion in the body which in turn would lead to more compulsive judgment. This process is how the passions ensnare us a thousand times a day. Tremendous forces flow through the heart. Out of habit, out of fear of the intensity, we contract into a small self that tries to manage it all—primarily through the thinking mind. We seek in vain to feel more of the good stuff and avoid feeling all the pain and sorrow that's present. This morning I could feel myself not wanting to be vulnerable to the magnitude of all that was in my heart. But as I realized I was gripped, I could let go each time and find a deeper willingness to think less and *feel more*.

I'm aware that the term *passion* can cause some confusion for the modern reader. To say that passion is a hazard in contemplative life can be confusing in a culture that all but equates passion with a life deeply lived. This confusion is merely a semantic issue. The passions, as I've been describing them here, point to a loss of freedom and agency when we become identified with thoughts and emotions that divide our heart, causing us to feel separate from ourselves, others, and the Divine.

In modern English, when we talk about living a passionate life, we're talking more about *enthusiasm*. Literally, enthusiasm points to being inspired by God and being full of Divine Energy. When we're enthused, energy flows and magnifies our sense of purpose. When we're ruled by the passions, however, energy freezes and our sense of self is captured by an acute sense of affliction. Rest assured, a life lived from the awakened heart does not ask you to give up the richness of feeling that makes life so worth living. Heart practice, if anything, teaches us to unfreeze the heart's fixations, an action that then allows greater vital energy to flow in ever-growing swells.

As we proceed, take this to heart: thoughts and emotions are just the very surface activity of a much grander realm that the heart is uniquely equipped to explore. Don't get too fixated on what emotions you're feeling in a given moment. Don't get too caught up in the content of your thoughts. As you learn to maintain steady contact with the Ground of your being prior to thoughts and emotions taking shape as a small, separate self, you will start to attune to the great broadcast that is constantly beaming from across the veil.

THE HEART AND MIND IN CONCERT

I had an experience years ago that has stuck with me. It changed the way I thought about the "mind," and it changed my belief about what kind of information we can receive when we live from the heart.

The experience was so ordinary. I was getting out of my car, heading to the gym to lift some weights (a dear pastime in my pre-dad life!), and suddenly, I felt the clear presence of a close friend of mine. I could see her face in my mind and even sense how she was doing in that moment. It was like she was right there. A second later, my phone rang. Of course, it was her.

I can't even remember what we talked about. That's my favorite part. She didn't call with life-altering news. It wasn't an emergency where she needed my help. She was just calling about some small thing. But in Marshall Mcluhan's words, the medium was the message that day.[6] In that moment, I consciously experienced myself, her, and all of us as intelligent cells in the One Heart—the great spiritual Field of Love and Intelligence.

When this event occurred, I was many years into my contemplative practice. I wasn't trying to meditate at the precise moment her presence appeared in my heart. But I had spent a great deal of time prior to that moment learning to attune to the Great Silence that is superabundant with Life, Love, and Light. I was beginning to experience these moments of *thinness* with more frequency. The boundary that seemed to separate me from others and the world itself often felt paper-thin. There was just something about the ordinariness of that phone call that brought it all together for me. Consciously, I realized and felt in my bones that everyone, everything, was *immediate*. That is, there was no distance that mediated between so-called me and everyone else. Everything, everyone, is present *right here and now*. In William Blake's words, "eternity is in love with the productions of time."[7] The intimacy and closer-than-close quality is hard to describe, but on that day, I felt like I got a glimpse of the scriptural wisdom that says, "They reside in the presence of God, on a globe like a sea of glass and fire, where all things for their glory are manifest, past, present and future, and are continually before the Lord" (Doctrine and Covenants 130:7). From that moment on, I realized in a deeper way that when I'm not totally enthralled by my wandering thoughts and sticky emotions, I become alive to past, present, and future all gathered in immediacy, all within the Sacred Heart.

To enhance this practice over the years, I've started to pay attention to what I call associative thinking versus spontaneous knowing. When we think associatively, we're operating from the mind's knowing. This practice is not a bad thing in itself, as I've tried to go out of my way to point out. But if we're stuck in this gear, we miss out on important spiritual realities.

For example, I drive by an old friend's home then start wondering how he's doing. Then I remember he now lives in Los Angeles and enjoys going boating with his family. Then I remember that one time he suggested we go boating with our kids. Then I remember that I'm really afraid of kids around water because two of my siblings almost drowned when I was young. Now I'm feeling anxious and starting to lengthen my outbreaths to soothe my nervous system a touch. I could go on and on like this, but you get the point. This example demonstrates a crucial way the mind works and makes meaning—through associative networks. Each sensory impression resonates through the mind and gets linked to similar experiences that may provide useful information for understanding what's happening in the present moment, as well as what might happen next.[8]

But if we're paying close attention, and particularly if we have some momentum in our practice of resting in the open heart, we observe some bits of information seemingly coming out of thin air. I've learned to pay special attention to this kind of activity because I know it's not stale information flowing along familiar mental-emotional channels. It comes by way of a different operating system altogether. It's not the thinking, associative mind, but the subtle heart, the spiritual satellite dish that's picking up on a broadcast from more lovely realms and realities. Whatever the content of the actual message, I find this quality of energy-information is often edifying. At some level, it feels spiritually nourishing just to be aware of and receive this kind of communication.

As my sensitivity around this practice has matured, I've realized something that I believe the Prophet Joseph Smith knew quite well: the mind and the heart were meant to function together in unison. Recall the scriptural passage I mentioned in chapter two. When asking for further knowledge on the process of translation, the Prophet received the following revelation: "I say unto you, that you must study it out in your mind; then you must ask me if it be right, and if it is right I will cause that your bosom shall burn within you; therefore, you shall feel that it is right" (Doctrine and Covenants 9:8).

As mind becomes entrained with heart, both centers of Intelligence come more fully alive. Kabir Helminski, a Sufi master and sibling of our Christian tradition, writes intimately about the way our manifold spiritual faculties work in harmony:

> Beyond the limited analytic intellect is a vast realm of mind that includes psychic and extrasensory abilities; intuition; wisdom; a sense of unity; aesthetic, qualitative and creative faculties; and image-forming and symbolic capacities. Though these faculties are many, we give them a single name with some justification, because they are operating best when they are in concert. They comprise an intelligence that is in spontaneous connection with the Universal Intelligence. This total mind we call, "heart."[9]

I want to draw particular attention to his insight that these faculties "are operating best when they are in concert."

Using the language you're now familiar with in this book, our spiritual Intelligence can take many forms and bring forth many qualities. If we're stuck in the "limited analytic intellect," revelation will be stymied. Caught in the loop of our habituated thoughts, nothing new can find its way in. If, on the other hand, we're stuck in the intuitive faculties of the heart, we might struggle to give shape and form to our inspiration. Yes, we'll feel beautiful Divine Light and Love, but what does God specifically want *me* to do with these gifts right now in this situation? The mind is our greatest ally in this territory. We can study out revelation in our minds. If our mind's knowing has fidelity to the revelation, our hearts will burn. The mind and the heart will be working in concert, and in this way God recruits us to go about the Holy Work.

Another inspired thinker, the great American psychologist William James, comments in this same vein: "Our normal waking consciousness . . . is but one special type of consciousness, whilst all about it, parted from it by the filmiest of screens, there lie potential forms of consciousness entirely different. . . . No account of the universe in its totality can be final which leaves these other forms of consciousness quite disregarded."[10]

This last sentence is so powerful: "No account of the universe in its totality can be final which leaves these other forms of consciousness quite disregarded." Or, if I can paraphrase, human beings can't truly be human until we are awake, alive, and embodied through all our faculties of spiritual Intelligence. From Helminski's "vast realms of mind" to James's "potential forms of consciousness entirely different," human beings, animated by Sacred Reality, have always intuited the vast Field of spiritual Intelligence to which we belong—our origin and goal at once. Parted from these divine realms of Intelligence by only the "filmiest of screens," the heart's knowing reveals the paper-thinness of these veils and the ease with which we can learn to travel from mansion to mansion.

To relate this all back to more familiar territory, this whole discussion hopefully represents an enriched understanding of what it means to follow the guidance of the Spirit, to live in the Spirit, and to allow it to guide our actions. Latter-day Saints have been living by this guidance since the foundation of the Church. Humans alike have been living by the Light of Christ since time immemorial. In the modern era, we're inclined to study things out in our mind, often bypassing the all-important process of grounding more deeply in the body, paying attention *from* the heart, and opening up awareness itself, like dilating the aperture of a camera to allow in more Light.

There are so many faculties we are not currently using. There are entire worlds beyond our normal waking consciousness. As the Restoration rolls forward, we are asked to see with new eyes still, to fully bring forth the gifts of the kingdom.

RADICAL REPENTANCE

I had a Living life with awareness flowing freely through a purified heart changes everything. It even changes something as fundamental as our relationship to repentance.

Traditionally, when we talk about repentance, we mean that a commandment has been broken and that we therefore need to get right with God by acknowledging what we've done, confessing the sin, feeling genuine contrition, making any amends necessary, and resolving to not commit the same sin again. There is real wisdom in this practice. The commandments mark very precisely where our appetites tend to run away with themselves and where we therefore need a certain amount of constraint. Repentance sensitizes us to our deep-seated inclination to act in ways that are harmful to ourselves and others. Repentance also reinforces our understanding that we can only be saved and perfected through Divine Love and Christ's Atonement.

There is a pitfall in this divinely inspired process, however. Namely, we risk cuing off a set of rules to gauge our spiritual health rather than risk a more radical transformation. Put bluntly, if we didn't knowingly lie, steal, or fornicate today, we may suppose that we have no occasion to confess our sins to God or to others. But the inner path is more subtle than this and asks more of us than to merely perfect our behavior. You may recall from the earlier retelling of the parable of the prodigal son that obedience to the commandments can become a mechanical act that fails to activate the deeper spiritual potential within all of us.

The principal transformative insight in the gospel I continue to point to throughout this book is this: the self we get caught up trying to perfect is actually the very self we're asked to take to the cross. In the words of Cynthia Bourgeault, "the true self can never simply be a cleaned-up, high-functioning version of the 'false self'."[11] By "false self," Bourgeault means the natural man and woman in each of us that relies on its own strength and merit. We are so attached to this false identity, so loath to give it up, we even attempt to convince ourselves that if we obey the law perfectly, we will one day stand blameless before God. But we can never be sanctified by systematically improving our behavior and attempting to be perfect. This path is no more than spiritualized egocentrism. We've merely replaced money, power, and things of the "world" with religious objects of desire: righteousness, piety, and salvation.

Worldliness in the gospel is decidedly not that aspect of human life which falls outside the purview of religion. We risk worldliness in the Church every bit as much as we risk worldliness outside the Church, sometimes even more so. From a transformative perspective, worldliness is any attempt to find security through finite means—safety, pleasure, the esteem of others, and the insatiable need to control our circumstances. The gospel invites us to leave this worldliness behind and find security in the only Reality that is worthy of our hearts. We are not sanctified by perfecting the false self but by waking up to an entirely new dimension of self, whose center of gravity is Christ.

In the New Testament, the Greek term *metanoia*, "repentance," points to exactly this process. *Meta* refers to "greater than or beyond," and *noia* comes from the word *nous*, which can mean "consciousness" but also connotes "self" and "identity."[12] Essentially then, we can think of *metanoia* as more than simply a change of heart or mind, although it very much is that. In the context of true transformation, *metanoia* is also going completely beyond our misunderstanding of who we really are.

The self we think we are is way too small to live a true life in the gospel. We're all way too absorbed in our projects of salvation, too anxious for our own honor. We neurotically try to improve this self so that when we reach the judgment bar, we are beyond reproach. None of this is wrong per se, but it misses the mark. It is a forgetting of who we actually are. Obedience, ironically, becomes sinful when it seeks to replace a genuine death of the self-that-we-are-not with religious performance.

Estranged from our Divine Source that alone confers value to all things, we obsess over building up a self and presenting it as an achievement. We would do better to recognize that the self is utter poverty if not for the Reality in which we live, move, and have our being (see Acts 17:28). To repent, then, is to become a "big self," a "true self." *Metanoia* is to continually go beyond the small self, opening ourselves to the vastness of God, to Divine Reality. Life, Love, and Light Supreme come to consume any pious notions we harbor of our own goodness. In true repentance, we see that Divine Reality is the very Goodness by which we are good.

I like to think about a "repentance-positive" lifestyle in this regard. When we're identified as the small, separate self, we don't like to admit we're in sin. We don't like to get caught learning. We want to appear to others as masters in all situations to avoid experiencing our own vulnerability. Repentance in this context is a painful, even humiliating, process that we like to avoid. We associate the process with failure and, as the small self, we hate to admit we've failed. But from a different perspective, we don't simply repent when we "break the law." We repent continually, day and night. Every time we feel ourselves contracting into a self that feels separate from others, separate from the world and separate from God, we practice expanding back into the fullness of the body, the radiance of the heart, the keenness of the mind, and the Light of open awareness. We reconcile ourselves with Divine Reality, and we atone. We practice being awake at all levels of our being to the sparkling Divine Reality in which we're completely immersed and which we ultimately are. This is the essence of repentance, the fuller meaning of *metanoia*.

When we repent with and through our entire being, we vulnerably open the self to God's Immensity. The experience can be intense, even painful, as I've described. But we can get used to this degree of Glory. This process of getting used to spiritual intensity should sound somewhat familiar to you by now! One of the great risks in contemporary spiritual life, one of the great sins, is that we try to *think* our way through the path, and we end up unconsciously defending against a much more radical, transformative process that God is eager to take us through. Repentance, in its more radical forms, is having the humility to admit that we actually have an impoverished idea of who we are and where we're going. Thomas Merton, a Trappist monk of the twentieth century, wrote:

> My Lord God, I have no idea where I am going. I do not see the road ahead of me. I cannot know for certain where it will end. Nor do I really know myself, and the fact that I think that I am following your will does not mean that I am actually doing so. But I believe that the desire to please you does in fact please you. And I hope I have that desire in all that I am doing. I hope that I will never do anything apart from that desire. And I know that if I do this you will lead me by the right road though I may know nothing about it. Therefore will I trust you always though I may seem to be lost and in the shadow of death. I will not fear, for you are ever with me, and you will never leave me to face my perils alone.[13]

What Merton portrays is deep repentance. We are so given to God that we've even given up the idea of our own worthiness. We can't even be sure if we're following the Divine Will exactly, even as that is our most sincere desire. But our heart burns within us. Paradoxically, God lights our way with a ray of darkness—with *unknowing*. We have faith that we are being guided, though we cannot know how or to what end.

If repentance and Divine Union are one indivisible act, then we can say that Jesus truly taught nothing and *did* nothing but repentance.

Of course, I'm not saying that Jesus sinned and therefore needed to be made right with the Law. But in the deeper sense of *metanoia*, he learned in his humanity, just as we do, to overcome the gravitational pull of the false self. When his human appetites and frailties groaned and pulled at his heart, he had to learn, just as we do, to open up his entire being to the Divine Reality, again and again. Through perfect repentance, he came to pray without ceasing. "Even though Jesus was God's Son, he learned obedience from the things he suffered" (Hebrews 5:8, NLT).

The small self naturally fears the path of crucifixion and resurrection. It gets flooded with anxiety and wants to have all the answers; it wants to know how it will all end in advance. If we're going to do radical repentance, we need to call on the subtle faculties of the heart. It's the heart, after all, that shows us we can let down our defenses. It's the heart that reveals to us that there are ultimately no true boundaries between our humanity and Divinity. To open up to this Immensity takes time. But we don't have to do more than we can do. It can start with admitting to ourselves that perhaps we've been pretending to know more than we actually know, that we've been trying to control things that are not actually ours to control. From here, we can let go into a bit more of a free fall. Like Merton, we don't need to see the road ahead, only to trust that God will never leave us.

SOME OF MY FAVORITE HEART-OPENERS

There are innumerable ways to better access the spiritual capacities of the heart. The following are a few of my favorites. You certainly don't need to take up every single practice here and do them daily for fifty years. Really, if even one of these practices opens something up for you, if it reveals the next step in your own growth, that would be more than enough.

As for the different practices below, I've noticed that as Westerners we like to have our options. It's nice when we're engaging in spiritual practice to be able to pick and choose a bit. The drawback to picking and choosing is that we might start to make a big deal of which practice is the best. We wonder, "Am I limiting my potential if I stay with only this one? Why don't I like that practice more than I do?" Keep it simple for now. Trust yourself. If it tastes good, trust your intuitive faculty to know Goodness and Truth. Your heart is *so big* already. However you feel guided, practice letting your heart be as big as it actually is.

MEDITATION
Heart Practice: Asking a Real Question

Learn to distinguish a mental-egoic thought driven by a sense of lack, driven by habit, as opposed to an impression that is totally surprising—even revelatory. This impression, this prompting, will be imbued with a sense of Power and Grace. It naturally inspires a sense of awe, love, and reverence.

In the Baha'i tradition, the Lord speaks to their prophet and says, "Thy heart is My home. Sanctify it for My descent."[14] In a sense, we're just learning to rest in the spacious, open silence of the heart, to purify it for the descent of the Spirit and its communications and to be willing to wait as long as it takes for authentic guidance to arrive.

INTRODUCTION
Lectio Divina

When I came back to Church after a long time away, I returned with a sensibility from the Buddhist tradition that meditation was both a foundational spiritual practice as well as a catalyst to deeper insight. Naturally, I was thrilled to discover the Christian practice of Lectio Divina (Latin for "Divine Reading") when I did. Not only did it enrich my scripture studies, but it also connected me to the rich history of Christian meditation that I'd never been exposed to growing up in the Church.

As you familiarize yourself with the practice, I think you'll find that there are elements similar to how we already work with scripture as modern Christians, but there are also novel elements that will likely bring you to new depths of Divine encounter.

MEDITATION
Read, Ponder, Pray, Rest

THE SACRED HEART | 105

A HEART OF FLESH

"A new heart also will I give you, and a new spirit will I put within you: and I will take away the stony heart out of your flesh, and I will give you an heart of flesh" (Ezekiel 36:26, KJV).

What a glorious prophesy from Ezekiel, anticipating the dawn of a new spiritual eon. What is the heart of stone that God promises to replace? I invite you to read, ponder, pray, and rest in this verse. See what the combined faculties of your body, heart, mind, and spirit can reveal to you about it. To me, a heart of stone is a heart that has grown crusty and stiff with the emotional habits of the small self. It is a heart afraid of risking itself for the sake of Eternity, preferring to remain enclosed in a false sense of security. It is a heart that sleeps to its true potential and divine endowment.

Krishnamurti, a great Indian sage of the twentieth century, once said, "When you teach a child that a bird is named 'bird', the child will never see the bird again."[15] In other words, the mental construct eclipses the dancing liveliness that we call "bird." We stop seeing the bird and see only our mind's opaque label. In my own life, more and more I see when I am covered by a sticky film of thoughts and beliefs about who I am and what life *means*.

In other moments when I'm seeing things more as they are in their infinite nature, my heart feels achingly attuned to Truth and Beauty. My heart is flesh again. My whole being is tender and responsive to Creation.

When our heart is soft, we spontaneously resonate with the spiritual aliveness of all things. It's something we often forget as adults, ever since we learned to project a mental map onto the world: "Oh, there's that *guy*. I don't like that guy." Or, "Today's *Monday*. I hate Mondays." We wear these labels like straitjackets in our lives. A practice of opening and activating the heart, of receiving a heart of flesh from our living God, is to return to our innocence and at-one-ment with all things.

I was in China recently, about an hour's drive outside of Beijing. My friend wanted to introduce me to her Tai Chi teacher. Master Yang was probably close to fifty years old with a shaved head, springy athletic build, and smooth face. He moved like a ribbon in the wind. His heart felt palpably awake to me. We were sitting in his teacher's quarters that flanked the courtyard where he practiced Tai Chi with his students. As he brewed a pot of tea, we were having an easy, friendly conversation. I said to him, "I'm experiencing something very interesting. I remember being in China when I was young. I was twenty years old when I first came here. It felt like such a scary, foreign place to me at the time. I felt worried all the time about how I was going to make money and just survive. Home felt so far away."

I tried to explain to him what a disorienting, vulnerable time in life that was for me, when I first showed up in China. I went on to say, "This time around, almost twenty years later, I come back and I feel like I'm *home*. Everywhere feels like home to me now. China feels like *home*." Master Yang imbibed my words like a perfectly brewed cup of tea. He seemed almost intoxicated by what I'd just said. He replied with a glint of delight in his eyes, "Ah, your heart has come down." I'd never heard those words spoken in Chinese, but I knew immediately what that phrase meant.

In the Chinese language and culture, the "heart" and "mind" are one single character: 心. When the heart "comes down," it means we actually drop awareness down from the thinking mind that is labeling everything: *China is scary. Home is far away.* Our center of gravity comes down into the heart, into the heart of flesh, and suddenly everything looks new. The boundaries that separated us from everything and left us feeling alone and exposed soften. They can even disappear entirely. The world takes on a vibrant and luminous quality. Everywhere we go is home when we live from the heart.

THE SACRED HEART | 107

MEDITATION
Knowing from the Heart

HEART YOGA

This next practice I call "heart yoga." If you've done yoga asana before, where you move sequentially through different physical postures, you'll notice that after a session, the body feels very expansive and energized, vibrant and limber. "Heart yoga" works this way on a more subtle level.

Have you ever noticed how powerful the words "I love you" feel when you say them? Not only powerful, but vulnerable. When you say these words, you open yourself up to the *sacred other* to express your love, but you also simultaneously risk being wounded, even rejected.

When we pay attention to this, we notice the experience can be quite *intense*, and as a result, we have a lot of strategies to avoid saying these words. In this heart yoga, we're making use of the fact that "I love you" tends to carry an intense charge with it. It feels risky and vulnerable to say. Therefore, it's a subtle posture of the heart we're stretching into. Being totally present and embodied, we say it and we notice the stretch. As we would say in yoga asana practice, we're using the yoga posture to *move into sensation*. In *heart* yoga, we're using the words "I love you" to grow into a greater measure of Divine Love.

MEDITATION
Heart Yoga

COME WHAT MAY AND LOVE IT

The final practice in this chapter was inspired by my grandparents. And to begin, I'd like to invoke the previous practice of heart yoga by saying, I love you, Grandma and Granddad. I want to express how much you mean to me and how much love you taught me.

I remember my Granddad Wirthlin's words in his final conference address in 2008. I was stopping through town in between tours of China and Europe. I had an opportunity to go hear him speak live at the Conference Center in downtown Salt Lake City. The name of his talk was "Come What May and Love It." The moment felt very full of Grace to me because even in the times where I felt quite exiled from my family and my community, I never felt exiled by my Wirthlin grandparents. I always felt a steady heart connection from them both.

As I relaxed into the flow of his address that autumn afternoon, I marveled at how familiar it felt to me. I'd been a practicing meditator for ten years at that time. His talk was dripping with the quality of *willingness*—what I would call *equanimity* in a Buddhist context. He taught that if we can be fully open and awake to experience as it is in this moment, it has a powerful, transformative effect in our lives.

I remember sitting in the congregation and being aware that I'd felt quite far away from home for a long time now. I'd felt unfriended, unMormoned. Yet here I was sitting in Latter-day Saint Mecca, listening to my granddad give a general conference address, and it felt perfectly like *home* to me. I felt I knew his heart perfectly. As he spoke, I knew with divine confidence that I had been doing my sincere best to cultivate the quality he himself was speaking of from such a mature place.

He pointed out how life is going to serve up all kinds of circumstances, many of them challenging, many of them the last thing we would have wanted. And yet, he said, we should respond with an attitude of "come what may and love it." Put another way, "whatever arises, love that." I was touched to feel his heart and hear him speaking the words he spoke that day.

He died just a couple months after giving that address. But after hearing that talk, I felt an assurance that we are family and maybe I'm not so far away from home after all. I love you, Grandma and Granddad. I feel you both alive and luminous right now, in the Sacred Heart that holds us all.

MEDITATION
Come What May and Love It

Chapter 5

Divine Vulnerability

A FEW YEARS AGO, my wife and I started working with a therapist who also happens to be a self-effacing Buddhist master named Bruce. Bruce is shinily bald and has wrinkled jowls that evoke the sleeves of a wizard. His eyes are clear and his gaze penetrating. When he laughs, there is nothing but laughter. He has an elegant way of getting to the heart of the matter with the kindness of a bodhisattva and the fierceness of a samurai.

My wife and I realized that there were some issues coming up in our marriage that we weren't easily going to resolve on our own. We needed additional skills and support. Personally, I felt relief that I could share some of my frustrations with a third party. Hopefully, I thought, my wife would be willing to listen to me better if a trained professional assured her that what I was saying was important.

In our first session, after a brief moment of pleasantries and introductions, Bruce asked us the therapist's equivalent to "what seems to be the problem?" I generously volunteered to go first and explain to him that there was a real sore spot in our marriage. "There are times when I'm really excited about something, really passionate, and of course the person I want to share that with is my wife. The problem is, I notice she gets distracted a lot when I'm sharing something that's really important to me. Sometimes it feels like she doesn't really care."

Bruce listened deeply, then reflected back, "I hear you saying that when you're sharing something that's really important to you, but then feel like your wife isn't fully present with you, it's a very disturbing experience."

"Yes, exactly," I said. "If I can't share my excitement about life with my wife, then who can I share it with?" At this point, only ten minutes or so into the session, I felt a whole-body sense of self-satisfaction. I'd articulated my frustration fully and someone had finally understood it. Now for checkmate—Bruce will explain to my wife how important it is to be a good listener, especially when I'm sharing something that means a lot to me.

Unexpectedly, Bruce put the question to me: "Thomas, I wonder if you'd be willing to give up the fantasy of a life free of disturbance."

My jaw must have involuntarily swung wide open like the overhead storage bin on an airplane during severe turbulence. A dead silence followed. I was stupefied. After I returned to my senses, a profound clarity hit me with no further explanation needed: I realized I had unconsciously made it my wife's responsibility to protect me from any disturbing experience in our relationship. I had told myself the fiction that if I was feeling disturbed, surely it meant that someone had done this to me and that it was their job to make me feel better. In a single deft stroke, Bruce had cut through my drama and revealed a completely different way to be in my marriage: my wounds, my disturbances were my own, and nobody else was responsible for them. (Of course he wasn't saying that when my vulnerabilities are triggered

I can't ask my loved ones for help. I can and I should. But if my go-to instinct is to blame people when I feel threatened, then I'm doomed to a life of constantly trying to control other people's behavior.) I was never the same after that moment. My wife assures me our marriage hasn't been the same either.

This is an example—a juicy one, I think—of an everyday disturbance. With the help of a highly skilled therapist, I was able to see that the disturbance of not feeling valued didn't start with my wife and therefore wasn't likely to end with her either. That pain in my life goes back to the foundations of human vulnerability itself.

From that moment on, I had an intention to stay curious each time I felt devalued. Rather than fixating on the story I had about how my wife needs to be a better listener, or how my friends ought to appreciate how helpful I am, I practiced staying in my body. I practiced staying with the very uncomfortable sensations that came up whenever I didn't feel esteemed and valued. In doing this, I've learned at least two important lessons. First, when I feel disturbed, the temptation to avoid responsibility and blame my discomfort on others is almost overwhelming. Second, with practice I can actually learn to rest in my vulnerability, letting intense experiences rise and pass through my body like waves. When I do this, after the intensity of the disturbance passes, I'm in a better position than ever to act with intelligent love, to do the most loving thing I can possibly do in the next moment.

THE DEVELOPING SELF

Bruce revealed to me through the therapeutic process how vulnerable I am in intimate relationships to not feel esteemed. To fully appreciate the range of what he calls "core vulnerabilities,"[1] it's helpful to first understand the developmental territory of our most basic biological needs. By definition, to have needs is to be vulnerable.

From the moment we're born, and indeed even before we're born, we have a need for the basic conditions of warmth, nutrients, and adequate rest. A newborn baby instinctually cries when she's too hot, too cold, hungry, or just plain tired. In addition, newborn babies are drawn to the voice, presence, and touch of their caregiver. If we leave a baby unattended for too long, or if a well-meaning friend or relative picks her up, she might show a range of distressed responses. Thus, from the very earliest stage of life, we start with a need for safety and security.

Just as foundational to our need for security is our drive to seek pleasure. In a sense, pleasure is a derivative of the conditions that ensure our safety and survival. For example, it's incredibly pleasurable to get a good night's sleep in a comfortable bed. It's pleasurable to eat delicious food and to have a healthy body that's free of any discomfort. Again, from before the time we're even born, this need to seek pleasure and avoid pain is innate to our biology.

Our sense of self starts to form from the moment we're born as well. As this "self" starts to form, "other" appears in relation to it. There is now a "me" and everything else that is "not me." This emerging self, tenuous in its individuation, is hungry for esteem and affection. From the first moments of our fledgling selfhood, we need to know that we're wanted. To state it in the negative, to not be wanted or not belong is to face certain death. Most adults wouldn't last too long left completely on their own in the wilderness. How much less an infant? Later in life we undergo a socialization process, and our relationships get more nuanced and complicated. But right at the heart of all human relationships is essentially a biological need to belong.

From about twelve to eighteen months in healthy development, we start to actively exercise our will and come into a sense of *power*. "I want that!" we yell from the top of our lungs. Wanting what we want, we're very clever at working out the best ways to get it. Sometimes we unleash the all-out charm offensive, overcoming mom or dad with blunt-force cuteness. Other times, we'll deploy the meltdown technique—kicking, screaming, and writhing until the caregiver surrenders. Not only do we learn to get what we want at this stage of life, we also learn to discern when we've met our match. We can tell when mommy means business and when we might push a little harder for some extra screen time or a lollipop. In other words, we learn not only control but submission. We learn when to bear down in an act of will and when to yield to a will more powerful than our own.

You can see from this brief tour of child development that these basic needs show up in the earliest stages of life. We are born completely vulnerable to the conditions of mortality. And to the extent that our needs are not perfectly satisfied each time one arises, especially in early life, we will feel a disproportionate level of disturbance as we move into adulthood.

CORE VULNERABILITIES

As long as we're an embodied human being, we will have foundational biological needs. When these needs feel threatened in any way, when we experience privation of any kind at this basic level, biologically the body has evolved to respond with a certain measure of panic. It sends us highly intense signals that our *very survival might be threatened*. We feel disturbed to our core.

I've got a nonhuman example, but I think a relatable one. Our neighbors have a rescue dog, Pfeiff (short for Pfeifferhorn), who we can speculate spent some of his early days on the streets, scrappy and hungry. He's now a thriving adult dog with loving caregivers. There's a catch, though. Our friends still need to keep the supply of dog food well out of Pfeiff's reach. Otherwise, he'll get into the bag and literally gorge himself until he's sick and throw it all up. We can imagine that Pfeiff spent so long being hungry as a pup—feeling as though he was at the brink of death—that the signals he gets when he's hungry to this day are especially intense, even exaggerated. Or in other words, he would do *anything* to avoid feeling hungry. Hunger pains, for Pfeiff more than most, mean imminent death. It's irrational—he's been food secure for many years now. All signs point to his next meal coming right on time, from two loving parents. But deep in his canine bones, he feels something very different from reality: *there is never enough*.

To some extent, no matter how loving or perfect our homes were where we grew up, we all have an inner "Pfeiff." We all experienced privation on some level, maybe even often. This experience is the nature of embodied life—we are vulnerable by design. At a biological level, we have basic needs that aren't always perfectly met.

None of us have any conscious memory of crying in our cribs as infants, the sting of hunger shooting lightning bolts of displeasure through our delicate frames. In those moments, we didn't have a mature mind that could reason, "Even if mom doesn't hear me crying, I'll just be a little uncomfortable till she wakes up. I'm not in any real danger." Rather, our direct experience was that we were on the brink of starving to death. The intelligence of our animal bodies produced an appropriately intense response, and as a result, we wailed with all our might to draw the caregiver close, to soothe the blaring sting in our world with the warm, fatty goodness of mother's milk.

From early life, the natural man (i.e., instinctual self) forms implicit memories of a world of lack. I mean "implicit" in the technical sense here—unconscious memories that are coded at the cellular level of the body. In our adulthood, these somatic impressions give rise to mental-emotional patterning that is primed for the experience of *not enough*. That is, we see through the eyes of mortal scarcity, and everywhere we look we see deficit. Let's review the developmental territory by looking at maladaptive responses to the core vulnerabilities one by one.

If I often felt a lack of security when I was young, I may be more prone to that experience later in life. Like Pfeiff, I might eat more than I need to at a given sitting to avoid the vulnerability I feel when I'm hungry. Or if my fixation takes a different pathway, I might be stingy with my resources, feeling deep in my body that I don't have enough to share with others.

Maybe I was deprived of pleasure or exposed to unbearable pain when I was too young to defend myself. Moving into adulthood, I might be prone to addiction, seeking pleasure and avoiding pain to an unreasonable degree. The ocean of suffering that seems to lie just beneath the thin surface of my everyday mind threatens to well up and drown me. As a result, I err on the side of pleasure-seeking to the point that I'm almost totally unwilling to have a direct relationship with pain.

If I felt deprived of esteem growing up, I might be especially vulnerable to seeking out affection and approval later on in life. The more I go looking for approval, the hungrier I get for it. It's actually very concerning to see the way social media exacerbates our vulnerability around esteem. It's now easier than it has ever been to get immediate visual feedback on how people feel about me: how many views or how many likes did my last video get? Captivated by this substitute version of true esteem, we risk losing touch with our innate and divine value.

And then the need for power. To whatever extent I didn't have the experience of being powerful in early development, I might fixate on the need to be in control later in life. Maybe my parents struggled to provide a proper holding environment for me when I was young. I never felt quite like I could control my own space. Now when I feel a loss of control in adulthood, I panic and look to control things I have no business trying to control—my adult kids, the real estate market, people's opinion of me.

Here I've emphasized the environmental, or nurture side, of vulnerability. But it's likely that we're each born with a biological predisposition to feeling certain vulnerabilities more than others. This is the classic nature/nurture dichotomy in psychology. Some of us may have more addictive personalities by nature and therefore react more intensely to the denial of a pleasure. Others of us who are more relational by temperament might be more vulnerable to a loss of esteem from others.

In any event, we have basic biological needs that are simultaneously our deepest vulnerabilities. We often react ineffectively to these mortal vulnerabilities in an attempt to escape our own suffering. Given this predicament, it would be convenient to have a language for this distinctly human psychology.

ENERGY CENTERS

In a brilliant move, Father Thomas Keating has integrated the developmental territory we just explored—core vulnerabilities and all—to life in the gospel. He realized that what Paul referred to as "lower nature" and the "natural man" can be understood not only theologically but psychologically as well.

Father Keating described this territory in terms of *energy centers*,[2] a term he adopted from the work of the author Ken Keyes Jr. The original metaphor is vivid. In physics, the center of gravity is the point in a body where the mass is concentrated. This mass, in turn, generates a gravitational pull. Gravitational fields can be weak or strong, depending on the mass of the body doing the pulling. We know from modern astronomy that gravitational fields can become so intense in the case of black holes that not even light can escape their field.

So it is with us mortals and our core vulnerabilities. The signals of the body can be so intense when these vulnerabilities are triggered, it is as if they exert a gravitational pull on our higher nature. When the signals are intense enough, they completely consume our attention, our Light in the vortex. We become fixated on the apparent emergency and routinely lose our capacity to make freer, wiser choices.

The energy centers in this sense are essentially one big energy suck. That is, when we're caught in the instinctual drives of the natural man, we invest our time, attention, and resources to escape the vulnerability we're *already feeling* in the body. We pursue symbols of security such as money and possessions in order to feel safe. We seek empty pleasures like scrolling on our devices and endless consumerism. We try to win the esteem of both ourselves and others by always being busy and constantly striving for accomplishment. We express a shallow sense of control by shouting over one another whenever we disagree. There is no end to these appetites. The more attention we feed these energy centers, the more massive they become. The more massive they become, the more difficult it is in each successive moment for us to escape their gravitational pull.

Because the body is developmentally foundational to our humanity, the heart and mind are especially vulnerable to its disturbances. Like any three-story building, if the ground floor has structural issues, the upstairs neighbors are going to feel it. Being aware of the activation of the energy centers helps us sense any tremors before they escalate into dangerous earthquakes on the upper floors. We learn to detect the very instant our basic needs feel threatened—when the shaking begins—and to seek more stable ground.

When we're not alert to what's happening in the body, before we know it, a disturbance has recruited energy from the mind and sent us into a flurry of anxious thoughts. The body then feeds on those thoughts and becomes even more disturbed. Or disturbance from the body seizes the heart and divides it with painful emotions. Those emotions then trigger similarly painful thoughts, thus agitating the body even more. In this way we generate our own private hell many times over in a single day.

As our awareness becomes more stable, however, we learn to soothe ourselves at the level of the body before these disturbances scatter the mind and divide the heart. How do we soothe ourselves? It is simple in concept but difficult to do in practice: we learn to be willing to feel what we're actually feeling in the body and to trust the Ground of our being. That might sound abstract, but it is actually extremely concrete. Lehi embodies exactly this trust when he speaks to his son Jacob in the wilderness: "Thou knowest the greatness of God; and he shall consecrate thine afflictions for thy gain" (2 Nephi 2:2). In more psychological language, as long as we are embodied beings, we are going to feel disturbance and signs of threat. But generally, the signs of threat aren't indicating any real threat. We just *feel* threatened. We can trust the body's process and let the tremors rise and pass without spinning elaborate dramas in the mind. When we're in our private hell, we think: "This isn't okay. I can't be here. I need out." When we're in heaven, it's just the opposite: "I *am* okay. This too is consecrated." This is freedom.

In summary, from the beginning of human life, we have basic biological needs. Because these needs are so foundational, any threat to them represents a threat to life itself. In this sense, our most basic needs are synonymous with our greatest vulnerabilities. The body, in its wisdom, sends us very intense signals of disturbance when our basic needs aren't met. The good news is that these signals help us stay alive and thrive. The bad news is that in modern adulthood, these signals are often out of step with objective circumstances. That is, we feel as though there's an emergency much more often than there actually is. Because the bodily disturbances associated with a perceived threat to safety, pleasure, esteem, and power are so intense, we develop a habit from a very young age of doing everything we can to escape feeling these disturbances. In this way, our natural biological disturbances become exaggerated into full-blown energy centers.

Recall my unconscious rationalization in marriage therapy: if my wife would just pay attention to me how I want, when I want, my need for affection and esteem wouldn't feel threatened and I wouldn't have to feel disturbed so often. In other words, rather than directly inhabit my vulnerability, I tried to control my wife's behavior in an ongoing fantasy that one day I would be free of any disturbance.

The moment we feel intense sensations building up in our bodies, our instinct is to escape. In an effort to escape the reality of our embodied vulnerability, we often say things and do things that are harmful to ourselves and to others. We justify our actions because we feel at a deep level that if we don't do something to escape, we'll be overwhelmed with pain, or possibly harmed beyond repair. In a gospel context, we can understand this psychological process as the drive toward *sin*.

SIN

The Greek word in the New Testament that we translate as "sin" is *hamartia*. It implies "to miss the mark, to err." But what mark are we missing when we sin? Where do we err in the vulnerability of these human bodies?

In a word, we risk worshiping the finite at the expense of the infinite. As human beings, we have basic needs that we can pursue endlessly in an attempt to avoid the basic fact of embodied vulnerability. There is nothing wrong with needing safety, pleasure, esteem, or power. In fact, we could say that these are all divine gifts we're given to enjoy in human life. The problem is, we are all too prone to getting sucked into those black holes. The energy centers chant only one mantra: "This is good, but I'd give it all for a little more." The appetite of our lower nature is insatiable. And because we can never get our fill at this level of reality, scarcity is the law of the land. In the passage from Lao Tzu that we glimpsed earlier,

> Fill your bowl to the brim
> and it will spill.
> Keep sharpening your knife
> and it will blunt.
> Chase after money and security
> and your heart will never unclench.
> Care about people's approval
> and you will be their prisoner.
>
> Do your work, then step back.
> The only path to serenity.[3]

What is purely irrational yet demonstrably true is that the more security we seek *beyond a reasonable point*, the more we feel like we don't have enough security. When we idolatrize our basic needs, they become hollow gods who are impotent to satisfy the true hunger of our souls. We're then left with the doomed task of trying to satisfy ourselves. In our worst moments, we'll justify any kind of behavior it takes to escape the specter of being swallowed alive by our core vulnerabilities. Sin in this sense is a vain but understandable attempt to avoid our deepest suffering.

In his formulation of original sin, St. Augustine duly notes our tendency to miss the mark, to act out. But he then goes a step too far in my opinion by imputing something corrupt about our humanity itself. With our new understanding of sin as a natural tendency to avoid vulnerability, we can easily imagine a new telling.

In a Latter-day Saint formulation of sin, we can start with a reverence for the physical body and an acknowledgement that our biological vulnerability brings with it certain liabilities. But these are precisely the liabilities we're given to work with in order to gain mastery over the physical realm. Vulnerability, in other words, is not a bug, it's a feature. We have the opportunity as embodied beings to willingly accept more and more vulnerability—both individually and collectively. As we bear one another's burdens, we imitate our embodied God who weeps, and we become more godlike ourselves in the process (see Moses 7).

The word *vulnerable* comes from the Latin *vulnus*, which literally means "wound." Thus, it is not sin and a corrupt nature that we've inherited as human beings but an original wound. By willingly embodying this Divine Vulnerability, we learn to descend below all things. To the extent that we're willing to not only endure but embrace our personal Gethsemanes, we curtail sin's capacity to tempt us. After all, if we're willing to feel absolutely every experience that the Divine consecrates for our sanctification, what need is there to act out? What power does sin have to tempt us in the end? Christ is the living incarnation of this path.

ENERGY CENTERS IN SCRIPTURE

Though we don't traditionally conceive it in such terms, there is a vivid depiction of the energy centers in the book of Matthew, chapter four. Jesus goes out into the desert in prayer and fasting for forty days. Many of us have read this story so many times, it's easy to skip to the end without letting the gravity of what is happening fully sink in. We know Jesus is tempted, we know he overcomes then emerges from the desert triumphant, declaring the good news. Let me slow us down a bit here and integrate what we know about the energy centers and how they play out in this scene. When I view this account through the lens of the energy centers, I see a clear path that Christ has shown us to further participate in our own theosis.

Whatever we personally take the devil to be, we can say that he is cunning. He knows right where to hit us. There Jesus is, out in the wilderness, hungry, alone, and weakened. The devil says to him, "If you are the Son of God, tell these stones to become loaves of bread" (Matthew 4:3, NLT). In other words, "feed yourself." Remember, the prime directive of the body is to get comfortable and to stay comfortable. We all know what it's like to be hangry. Few of us know how intense our disturbance would be if we fasted for days and weeks on end. This portion of the story depicts energy center number one: safety, security. The devil tempts and mocks him, as if to say, "You have all the power in the world. Why go hungry when you could have a bite of bread right now?" Jesus responds: "People do not live by bread alone, but by every word that comes from the mouth of God" (Matthew 4:4, NLT).

There is relative happiness, and there is happiness beyond conditions—the pleasure of having agreeable life circumstances versus the joy independent of circumstances altogether. Jesus is clear which master he serves and overcomes the first temptation.

In the second temptation, the devil takes Christ up to the top of the temple and says what amounts to, "If you're such a big shot, throw yourself off from this temple and all of the angels, all of your pals, will show up and they won't so much as let you stub your toe. They'll take care of you."

This portion of the story clearly touches on the energy center of esteem and affection. In this mode of temptation, the devil plays on the very human need to feel important, to feel that if anything doesn't go our way, we've got a posse at our back. Putting his trust in God alone, Jesus sees through this guile: "You must not test the Lord your God" (Matthew 4:7, NLT). In the third temptation, the devil pulls out all the stops. He takes Jesus to the peak of a very high mountain and shows him "all the kingdoms of the world and all their glory" (Matthew 4:8, NLT). Then the devil mocks Jesus yet again, saying, "I will give it all to you . . . if you will kneel down and worship me" (Matthew 4:9, NLT). In other words, "you could have power and dominion over all things, if you first submit to me."

Jesus knows, however, that if he seeks power, the seeking will never end. His heart will never unclench. He responds, "You must worship the Lord your God and serve only him" (Matthew 4:10, NLT).

This account was written nearly two thousand years ago, long before we had any sophisticated understanding of psychology in the modern sense. Yet the patterns remain timeless. Our core vulnerabilities are our greatest temptations. When our basic needs are threatened, we get intense signals from the body telling us there's an emergency. From there, we have a strong tendency to freak out and rush to a short-term solution to escape what we're feeling.

By overcoming each temptation, by confronting each core vulnerability of our humanity, Jesus chooses the only true happiness there is. How appropriate that his ministry should start right here in this moment of victory over the devil: "Jesus came to Galilee, proclaiming Good News from God. 'The time is ripe,' he said, 'God's realm is already so close to you. Turn towards it. Trust this Good News'" (Mark 1:14–15[4]).

In fact, the kingdom is closer than close. When we are no longer afraid of our own vulnerability, when we are at-one with the joy and sorrow of our embodied humanity, we find an entirely new center of gravity in Divine Reality.

Though perhaps not as dramatic as the scriptural account, we are faced with similar temptations in the desert every day of our lives.

To view the modern desert of temptation, look no further than the string of billboards lining the freeways. Almost without exception the messaging is designed to amplify our innate sense of lack. The advertisements tell us we would be happier if we made more money working from home, looked more beautiful by getting plastic surgery, had a drink while surrounded by beautiful people of influence, or went to the Bahamas to unplug.

How are we doing in our own desert? How often are we driven to satisfy the insatiable needs of the energy centers? Are you starting to see now that there is a part of you that will never feel safe and secure enough? A part of you that will never feel enough pleasure and avoid enough pain? There's a part of you that cannot be adored enough no matter how many friends and admirers you have. The task is simple but difficult: Let your eye be single to God's Glory. Let this sanctifying Light infuse the most vulnerable parts of yourself again and again. In exactly the most disturbing moments of your life, you can train yourself to open up, relax, and trust that something from beyond is making you holy.

OUR NEW NATURE IN CHRIST

One of the central dramas in the New Testament is that between the old self and the new self, between the creature of sin and the creature that is made new in Christ. Paul writes plainly of this struggle in his letter to the Romans:

> I love to do God's will so far as my new nature is concerned; but there's something else deep within me, in my lower nature, that is at war with my mind and wins the fight and makes me a slave to the sin that is still within me. In my mind

I want to be God's willing servant, but instead I find myself still enslaved to sin...My new life tells me to do right, but the old nature that is still inside me loves to sin. Oh, what a terrible predicament I'm in! Who will free me from my slavery to this deadly lower nature? Thank God! It has been done by Jesus Christ the Lord. He has set me free. (Romans 7:22–25[5])

What does it mean that our "lower nature" is at war with our mind and makes us a slave to sin? The view of the energy centers model is that each time our basic needs even *appear* to be threatened, at some primordial level, the body panics. Let me emphasize that rarely do we *consciously* experience this panic. It is much more common at a conscious level to find ourselves casually seeking pleasure and rehearsing familiar stories about how we're right and others are wrong. But the panic is real. So often when we believe we're making free decisions, we're covertly doing everything we can to quell the intense signals coming from the body. We're seeking more of whatever quality we're convinced is missing. Repentance, conversely, is a reorientation of our entire being towards the divine realm.

Christ has walked this path. He has made peace with the core vulnerabilities of human-divinity, His and ours. He has subdued the appetites that would enslave us and steal energy from our higher nature. Christ has done this, as I see it, not only *for us* but *as an example* to us. He asks us to walk the path with Him.

Our lives, too, are a desert of temptation. Yet each time we bring our highest awareness, our purest love to our own wounds and to the wounds of others, we are directly participating in the process of atonement. We are sanctifying the body of flesh with the Light of awareness and participating in the risen life of Christ and His Virtue.

In Liberty Jail, the Prophet Joseph suffered at the hands of his captors and cried out in despair for God's mercy. God's response to him then is the same to us now: "The Son of Man hath descended below them all" (Doctrine and Covenants 122:8). It is the nature of Christ—of Sacred Reality—to descend below all things in order to redeem all things by and through perfect Love. Through Christ's universal and unrelenting Love for His Creation, we too can learn to love our vulnerabilities and those of others—not trying to escape from them but escaping *into* them, anointing the incarnate world with Divine Mercy.

EXAMPLES OF THE ENERGY CENTERS FROM EVERYDAY LIFE

Below I'll offer some examples of the energy centers from my personal life. As a transformative practice, you can be on the lookout from now on in your own life when these core vulnerabilities show up, especially when they start to take up more of your time, energy, and attention than they actually deserve. As a general rule of thumb, anytime you catch yourself being overly busy, scattered in your mind, looping a familiar story in your head about how you've been wronged, you can stop and ask, "Is there a deeper vulnerability in the body right now that I'm unwilling to feel?"

In time, we learn to unwind the habit of feeding these primal drives, always feeling as though something's wrong with this moment, always feeling that we have to struggle in order to secure what's missing. We learn to operate in our higher nature, a place that by definition is one of spiritual abundance: I have more than enough right now. I'm okay exactly as I am. I might not prefer to feel what I'm feeling in this moment, but at a deeper level, I know there is a process of purification going on that I can trust. I feel Christ's redeeming Love.

Safety

I've mentioned many times now my love for contemplation—sitting in stillness and resting in *Beingness*. Having sat in silent meditation for many thousands of hours in my life, I've gotten really familiar with what kinds of thoughts tend to pop up out of the silence. I've observed the content and frequency of different kinds of thoughts more times than I can name. And for me, I notice fairly often that when I'm at rest, my mind boots up and starts to churn out thoughts related to money: "How's my organization doing? Do we have enough money to comfortably make it through the year? That last event we put on was more expensive than I'd anticipated. Did we cover our margins?"

Beneath all of these thought forms is the stirring of a familiar emotion: I'm afraid I'm not going to have enough. The anxiety of not having enough is distinctly unpleasant. I don't like to feel it. Therefore, it's tempting to obsess over whether I have enough, to believe I don't have enough, and to act like I don't have enough by being less generous with my resources.

These are some of the contours of my personal worries around safety and security. They're not always gnawing at me, but when I get really quiet and look close, I sometimes feel the rumble of this energy center in the depths. In these moments, I've learned the healthiest thing I can do is to go directly into the challenging sensation and remain open. It's counter-instinctual—that is, it's not what I want to do. But if I'm willing to feel this disturbance, it teaches me at an even deeper level that I am fully resourced no matter what sensations I'm feeling in a given moment of life. I can remain in God's rest. This is actually true abundance: no matter what life's circumstances are, no matter what discomfort is erupting in the body, at the deepest level, I can know that Divine Reality will provide for me.

Pleasure

I grew up with a lot of brothers—five brothers and one sister to be exact. We were like a pack of wolves, my sister being the toughest pup in the litter.

One Sunday during my weekly visit to my parents' home, I am having dinner with all but two of my brothers there. My mom has baked her signature, made-from-scratch dinner rolls. It's an old recipe she's been perfecting her whole life. People in the neighborhood know about these rolls. They're a big deal.

There we are, gathered around the table. The smell of freshly baked rolls, right out of the oven, wafts across the kitchen and dining room. We all salivate like Pavlov's dogs. After filling up my plate with crisp greens, buttery mashed potatoes, and whatnot, I enjoy the first few bites of a sumptuous Sunday meal, taking all the time in the world to thoroughly chew and delight in each bite—the mindfulness teacher that I am. With my appetite now properly whetted, I'm ready to load up on the main prize: a hot roll with melted butter and just enough homemade strawberry jam that it oozes over the sides. Only, I look up, and to my horror, there are just a few measly crumbs where a heaping mound of homemade rolls was steaming just moments before. My savage brothers had eaten two, even three, apiece before I could get to them. From one moment to the next I plunge from heaven to hell.

Rationally speaking, I knew I wasn't going to starve to death. I had plenty of food on my plate and plenty of fat on my bones. But I had been denied a supreme pleasure. The beast I keep carefully locked up within me raged. I remember wanting to yell at and shame every last filthy animal gorging themselves at that dinner table.

Familiar with my animal nature, I felt this energy center activate, and in lieu of scolding my siblings, I went deeper into the disturbance and just breathed. After the initial wave of reactivity passed, I regained my adult capacities and went about eating undramatically.

The simple taste of *Being* gradually returned, more delicious than any baked good.

Esteem

I mentioned earlier that when I was a young teenager, I lost all will and desire to attend Church. It was scandalous to my family and community. But for the life of me, I couldn't get myself to go. The more my parents pushed me, the more the situation devolved into a battle of wills.

Adolescence is plenty disorienting and awkward in the best of situations. But when I look back on that period in my life, the most painful element of it by far was feeling like I'd lost the esteem of my parents. Not only that, but my safety felt threatened when I started feeling like I didn't belong in the family anymore. I thought, "If I don't belong with my own family, where on earth do I belong?"

That experience of losing esteem and affection led to a nearly constant, low-grade panic. Within two years of dropping out of the Church, I'd developed clinical depression and a debilitating anxiety disorder. I didn't sleep well at night, and I couldn't begin to find my way through the dense brain fog during the day. Through junior high and high school, I performed worse and worse in school. Along the way, I lost a lot of esteem for myself.

After a tortuous five years of battling mental health issues, I started practicing meditation. It took me years to develop any real competency at it. But in hindsight, it was through the practice of still sitting that I developed one of the most important life skills I've ever learned. Slowly, gradually in the stillness, I learned to trust my own basic goodness. I can't explain to you exactly how it happened. I think the process is different for all of us. But in the expansive darkness I encountered on my cushion, I started to intuit a quality right at the heart of my being that was good. Not my own goodness, but Goodness itself was good. And somehow, I knew that I participated in that Goodness. Later I came to recognize that Goodness as Christ, the one who helped me remember my own soul's worth.

Power

The energy center of power is alive and well in me too. Talk to my wife about how I act when my computers freeze. I click on something, I want to do some simple task on my computer, and the dreaded spinning wait cursor appears—the beach ball of death. Almost immediately I melt into a whimpering puddle. "Not today. Any day but today. Why me?"

I know this experience is the epitome of a first-world problem. I'm not proud of it. But there you have it. Objectively, I know there's nothing life-threatening or inherently insulting about a computer taking its time to perform a task. But something in my animal body feels otherwise. When I see that beach ball, my intestines curl up in knots, and I want to EXPLODE.

My tech-rage was a big enough issue—basically consisting of me cursing fecklessly at the computer screen until I was emotionally exhausted—that I decided to really take it head on. I was getting so disproportionately angry when my technology would stall, I knew that my reactivity could only be covering up a deeper vulnerability.

When I really dove deep into the experience, I had an insight: Something in me feels *completely helpless* when my technology doesn't work. I feel a loss of control, and an inexplicable grief starts to bubble up from the depths, as if from a subterranean pool of poison. I feel as though life is passing me by, that I'm squandering my time, my one precious life. Intuitively, the grief is tied to the painful time in my adolescence when I felt stalled. The beach ball symbolizes lost time, lost opportunities to the traumatized teenager in me. At a deeper level, feeling like I've lost time brings up feelings of worthlessness in me.

And when I go even beneath that story, there is only *open vulnerability, without form or reason.*

After seeing me go ballistic enough times, my wife was kind enough to point out to me that that didn't seem to be helping the problem. Her reflection helped me redirect my attention from emotional reactivity to the deeper vulnerability. Deeper than even the personal history I pieced together in connection with the beach ball, I learned to stay more with just the raw sensations coming up in the body: a slight vertigo from a sudden loss of blood to the head, throat constricting, fists clenching. The energy was incredibly intense. But I trained myself to stay with the raw energy a bit longer each time.

To this day, I still feel a charge when technology jams up on me, but that charge no longer drives me to act out in the way it once did. I've learned through practice that feeling utter helplessness and vulnerability in the body from time to time is not necessarily an emergency. If I don't get lost in my emotions and interpretations of what's happening, thus pouring gasoline on the dumpster fire, I find the sensations well up and subside much more quickly than they ever did before. Not only that, but they leave a wake of peace behind them now. Once the great bane of my existence, the beach ball is now a call from Grace to even deeper embodiment.

RIGHT RELATIONSHIP WITH THE ENERGY CENTERS

Life is actually disturbing us all the time. It's provoking us all the time at the level of our basic vulnerabilities. We think if we use more force, more cunning to get conditions back to a place where we don't feel so upset, then we'll finally be okay. In fact, this agenda is a program for misery. As long as we are unwilling to feel the vulnerability we're *already* feeling, there will be no end to how much we struggle to escape our current experience. The energy centers will grow more massive and devour even more of our Light as they do so.

As long as we are sensitive, embodied beings, we will feel disturbed on and off for the rest of our lives. This is the reality Bruce had in mind when he asked me with a Zen master's sternness if I would be willing to give up my fantasy of a life free of disturbance. God wants us to get the message too. We are vulnerable in our humanity. We will be constantly tempted to blunt what we're feeling by acting out and engaging in short-term strategies that make us feel a little better now but a lot worse in the long-run. It's sin by any other name.

Remember that in a sense, sin is a wrong view that denies Divine Reality and the abundance that *is already right here.* Sin is what feeds the energy centers and our chronic sense of lack. More than a punishable act, sin is a lost opportunity. Think of the last time you did something you would consider to be sinful, whether big or small. Were you not avoiding some uncomfortable experience in the body, doing something that you thought would bring you a little bit of relief in the moment, only to realize that acting out made things even worse than they were before?

The more we respond to the energy centers with a conviction that we must escape from what we're feeling, the more we'll come to believe that we aren't capable of embracing our original wounds with love and acceptance. The more we act out from the energy centers, the more we reinforce the aspect of our humanity that feels alienated from God.

When we relate to the energy centers from a new place, however, they become a passageway into Grace. Every time we crash, every time we fall apart, we can stop and realize that this is an opportunity to be tender and fully embodied with this disturbance, with the most vulnerable parts of our humanity. As we do this, we discover exactly where we stand in need of healing. We feel our wounded humanity being redeemed.

Paul wrote, "What a terrible predicament I am in! Who will free me from my slavery to this deadly lower nature? Thank God! It has been done by Jesus Christ, the Lord. He has set me free."

God uses time and mortality to create beings who can withstand Eternity. The Love, the Light, the sheer energy of Eternity is so immense, it takes time to get used to it. We have to get used to the intensity of true joy as well as the intensity of our disturbances. The energy centers show us precisely where we collapse. What feel like the most awful aspects of mortal life are actually Grace Absolute in disguise. The energy centers are like spiritual growth plates. They're right where our soul is yearning for further expansion.

What's more, when we learn to stay present to our own disturbance, we learn to stay present to all disturbance. In the end, it doesn't matter if it feels like "my" disturbance or "your" disturbance. Disturbance is simply disturbance. It is a form of contracted Love, hidden in the shadows yet still seeking the Light.

We are Love's means. Christ didn't simply carry out the at-onement once and for all; He showed us how to at-one each moment of our lives through great acts of Love. When we are at-one with disturbance—the pain and vulnerability of our human-divinity—we redeem one another in Holy Presence. Bringing a greater measure of Love, a higher intensity of Light to disturbance, to the inclination towards sin, we heal the human family as Christ's true body.

MEDITATION
Exploring Your Own Energy Centers

We have our own vulnerable humanity and lower nature that we're enlisted to heal with Christ's help. We're invited to allow Grace to redeem us on the disciple's path. But as we get into the practice, we realize it's not just our energy centers or our impulse towards sin that we must be aware of. We come from families, we come from communities, we come from societies, cultures, and nations. The same energy centers are present throughout. They move in patterns. A given family, for example, will struggle with one energy center more than another.

I think about my Wirthlin grandparents who embodied the spirit of pioneer frugality. With that mindset, you don't just throw out foul-smelling bacon grease—you can still lubricate the handcart wheels with it! They were always conscientious about how they were using resources for the greatest good. In addition to bearing the pioneer spirit, they also came of age during the Great Depression where the experience of material scarcity must have been very intense. I can't know for sure, but speculatively it makes sense to me that some of their innate dispositions mixed with unique cultural events. This combination might have given rise to not just an impulse to be responsible with their resources but perhaps some anxiety around not having enough at times.

In any event, I began to notice later in life that whenever our family made a significant purchase, my mom's anxiety would spike. I then began to notice even later in life that I would get anxious whenever my wife and I would go out to eat more than once a month. Something deep inside me told me it was extravagant to eat out so often—that if we kept doing that, at some point we would run out of money. *There won't be enough!*

It's all just a story, but I have a sense that in my particular family, we have a few kinks to work out with the energy center of safety and security. In modern terms, we often translate safety and security as, "How much money do I have? Is it enough?" Note that this is not a conversation about how much money we objectively have so much as what our relationship to money is. This practice asks us if we can let money come and go without stickiness. It asks us if we can be comfortable when God gives us much and trust in God when times are lean. In my view, this is a very advanced practice. It's an area of continual growth and continual disturbance for me personally.

Here I am generations away from crossing the plains and living through the Great Depression. Objectively, I have way more than I need to take care of my family's and my own material needs. Objectively, I enjoy more material abundance than almost any human being to have ever lived on this planet. I've got a grocery store down the street, a climate-controlled home, a warm shower whenever I want one—and yet this same pattern of scarcity runs through me, across the generations.

These reflections are not about blaming anybody. We're all human, all working with our basic needs and vulnerabilities. In my opinion, as humans, we're all a little freaked out by the situation we're in on some level. Life is hard, serving up one intense experience after another. Who among us doesn't have an array of avoidant strategies for not feeling the full force of embodied life? In fact, as we become more honest about our own disturbances and the ways we avoid them—by casting blame on others, getting reactive emotionally, hiding in compulsive thinking, or always finding ourselves "busy"—we start to feel much more compassion for the way others are acting out. Because we're not in denial about our own wounding, we can be nonjudgmental about how others cope with their own wounding.

I've been really humbled in this practice to realize that when I heal from the need to escape my own wounded humanity, I'm not the only one being healed. As Christ heals me and makes me more whole, this Wholeness reaches backwards and forwards in time simultaneously. Wholeness itself increases. This Wholeness in Christ heals previous generations who weren't nearly as fortunate as I am in my current circumstances. The unfulfilled yearnings of my ancestors feel as though they find resolution.

In my move to Boston on a cross-country road trip, I stopped in Winter Quarters, Nebraska. When I was overlooking the cemetery where so many bodies, young and old, were laid to rest, I felt an upwelling of the most sublime Sorrow I've ever known. I lost all my bearings and could only feel consuming pain and grief in every direction. Suddenly in that tempest, I felt an impression as a sharp ray of Light that I can only attempt to translate into words: "We need you to feel this *in your body*. It was too much for us at the time, but you can help us feel this now." Somehow I was given to know in that moment that keeping myself open to the pain and suffering of my ancestors was Holy Work. *Divinity seeks embodiment endlessly in order to be all things and to know all things.* In the depths of Sorrow, I experienced Sacred Joy for the privilege of being in communion with fellow Saints from across the veil and bearing a small part of their burden with them.

By that same spiritual reality, as I inevitably fail to fully metabolize the painful experiences of my own life, I have a prayer in my heart that my grandchildren's grandchildren will take up my unfinished work. I hope by any healing I've been graced with that my children will start with a greater sense of Wholeness than I knew growing up. I hope that my soul's migration towards Wholeness will support their capacity to become more whole in Christ than any generation before.

It's all to say that we're never doing this work alone, or exclusively for ourselves. To the extent that we can practice Divine Vulnerability in our own bodies and open to the unresolved pain of family, community, and world—we continue the work of healing. The more we can bring full awareness and compassion to our collective woundedness, the more these aspects of our One Body are transformed by Sacred Love.

REFLECTIVE JOURNALING:

Below are some journal prompts to get you reflecting more deeply on the energy centers, both individually and collectively. Read the following questions, and take some time to write about them. In addition, you can find a trusted friend or partner to discuss these questions with. The intention is to bring greater awareness to these patterns and to work with the energy centers in a more inspired way as you see them come up in daily life.

- *When you feel disturbed, is there a particular energy center that seems to be at play? Safety/security, pleasure, esteem/affection, or power?*
- *Do you notice a pattern in your life where some vulnerabilities seem to be activated more often than others?*
- *Which energy centers are asking for your attention to be healed, to be held in loving kindness, to receive more Grace?*
- *What about patterns in your family? Are there patterns moving in your family that have been unconscious until now that you can bring more kindness, more caring awareness to?*
- *In your religious community, are there energy centers that are active, that you can bring more kindness and healing awareness to?*
- *What caring awareness does the entire world call for? What energy centers seem to be active and buzzing on the planet at this time? How can you be the Love that helps soothe our collective wounds?*

ON OBEDIENCE AND DIVINE VULNERABILITY

In theory, the practice of obedience invites the Spirit to be with us and to continually transform us into greater and greater expressions of our human-divinity. Obedience in its pure form is an alignment with true principles and spiritual patterns that guide us toward becoming what we're meant to become. It can be surprising, then, when we realize that obedience is sometimes a symptom of our insatiable desire towards safety, pleasure, esteem, and power. Ironically, to be perfectly obedient can mean to be in perfect sin. It comes down to the question of motivation.

Jesus knew the energy centers well and cut to their root: "If anyone comes to me and does not hate father and mother, wife and children, brothers and sisters—yes, even their own life—such a person cannot be my disciple" (Luke 14:26, NIV).

This scripture is one of the so-called hard sayings of Jesus. But if we understand the energy centers, it need not be hard. In light of the insights from this chapter, the teaching might sound something like this: "If you value the esteem of others over the truth of *who you really are*, you will be serving another master entirely. As for your life, if you value safety over dying to the self that you never were to begin with, you will never come to know the resurrected life."

From the perspective of ongoing progression and transformation, we can't just hunker down and obey the rules. The gospel asks us to give up the fantasy of comfortable transformative change. The very mentality that we can secure salvation through perfect obedience is itself a fantasy derived from the natural man and woman.

We tend to think of church as the place we go to overcome our animal drives, the appetites of the natural man and woman. But our lower nature has no trouble at all taking up residence in religious life and refusing to yield to a more vulnerable life in Christ. Here, just like everywhere else, we can learn to fit in, say all the right things, enjoy the admiration of the community, and feel as though we're in perfect control of our own salvation. Ironically, church might be one of our favorite places to hide from the disturbing process of transformation in the end.

True religion, on the other hand, is *metanoia*. It is perfect repentance. Recall from the previous chapter that the root meaning of *metanoia* is "to go beyond the self." That is, to go beyond our lower nature, to source our motivation from a new Reality. When we *go beyond*, we look for happiness in an entirely new direction.

When Jesus emerged from the desert, having healed from any need to escape his vulnerable humanity, He had fully entered the logic of the kingdom. He taught repentance, not because we should be ashamed of our depraved humanity but because it is and always has been God's good pleasure to give us the kingdom, if we only had eyes to see. This is the good news!

To feel what we're given to feel and act from a place of freedom and love is to practice Divine Vulnerability. In a given situation, maybe we feel inspired to do nothing, or maybe we offer up our spirited resistance to shift the outcome. The crux of the matter is not whether we take action or not. Rather, it is the quality of Presence and motivation we bring to each moment of engagement. Are we free to act as a divine being, or are we compelled to act as a wounded animal backed into a corner? Our lower nature will always seek as much safety, pleasure, esteem, and control as possible. Our new nature in Christ naturally *rests* in Infinite Being, feels a *fullness* of Joy irrespective of life's conditions, *trusts* in God's Love, and readily submits to the Divine Will.

We are born vulnerable, not sinful. We are wounded, not estranged from God. We are born with basic human needs that will not always be perfectly met. When a sense of lack threatens to overwhelm us, we are prone to acting out and missing the mark. In our worst moments, we will say anything and do anything to escape the feeling of being swallowed up in our pain. In the end, our sin is nothing more than a misguided attempt to escape from our greatest suffering.

Christ would have us be whole. He would heal us from our need to escape vulnerability and teach us the way of Divinity by fully embracing the wounds of all worlds. In this way, our weakness becomes strength. He calls our vulnerable humanity to fall further upward in the Gravity of Love.

The gift of physical embodiment is that it offers us real-time training in One-ing with the full spectrum of Creation. The body-heart-mind is a hands-on school of Divinity that teaches us to consciously join Spirit with matter (see Doctrine and Covenants 131:7), thus growing in our capacity to know Joy. Just as Christ went to the heart of the earth after His Crucifixion, we can descend to the depths of incarnation continually, redeeming what is dark and what sleeps in the saving Light of Divine Reality.

MEDITATION
Practicing Unconditional Kindness

SECOND INTERLUDE

The Infinite Self

IN THE FIRST INTERLUDE, I suggested that our ideas and beliefs about who we are constitute a very narrow aspect of our true identity. The inner path is all about embodying more of our fullness and, in time, coming to know ourselves as an always-transforming being.

Jesus said to Nicodemus, "I tell you the truth, unless you are born again, you cannot see the Kingdom of God" (John 3:3, NLT). Nicodemus responded, bewildered: "What do you mean? How can an old man go back into his mother's womb and be born again?" (verse 4). His confusion is not so different from our own.

How *can* we be reborn? How do we become a new creature in Christ? According to the transformative practices I've been describing throughout this book, full embodiment is a necessary element in this holy alchemy. As our minds wake up and become single, we learn to abide in greater Light. As the heart becomes pure, Divine Love reveals itself to be both our substance and salvation. As we become more willing to submit to the full range of anguish and ecstasy in our physical tabernacle, we experience Life more abundantly.

If this were all—increasing our capacity to know Divine Life, Love, and Light by exercising body, heart, and mind—it would be an authentically powerful path. But there is an additional *developmental dynamic* in the reality of *at-one-ment* that opens an evolutionary dimension in our human-divinity.

Eliza Snow, preeminent poet of the Restoration, points to a mystery that Latter-day Saint theology articulates with unusual clarity. In an intimate conversation with her Heavenly Parents, Snow wrote:

> In thy holy habitation,
> Did my spirit once reside?
> In my first primeval childhood
> Was I nurtured near thy side?[1]

"Primeval childhood" is an arrestingly beautiful phrase that should give us pause. It stands alone, as far as I know, in all of the Christian tradition. Historically, the predominant view among diverse Christian denominations is as follows: Humans were with God in the garden of paradise, there was a Fall (a calamity, in fact), then an intervention—Christ's Atonement—that allowed humanity to recover its original state. We could now return to the paradise where we started. The resulting formula becomes as follows: Creation, Fall, Atonement.

Latter-day Saint theology is more nuanced and developmental in nature than this traditional account. In the telling of the restored gospel, all prehuman intelligences were organized as discrete spirits by loving Parents who intimately understood the path of full embodiment. They prepared a way for us to develop into the full stature of our Divinity, just as They took on physical bodies to realize Their own Fullness. We became Their spirit children through Their compassionate embrace of our inchoate being. Later, in our primeval childhood, we chose the difficult path of earthly life in order to advance in our progress as gods and goddesses.

Embodiment, therefore, is not an unfortunate accident or state of affairs we learn to cope with until we get back to the good stuff. Embodiment is the essence of Divinity (see Doctrine and Covenants 93:33). It *is* the good stuff. This very body, heart, and mind, the very Spirit-substance that is living and breathing and comprehending the words on this page, this is the leading edge of your human-divinity and the Divine Life we all share collectively through our consecrated relationships.

The circular formula of creation, fall, and atonement becomes a spiral of always-widening rings, repeating in an endless progression. *Creation* occurs at each and every new stage of maturity—a new self and world is born. We *fall* out of one paradise as we become ready to embody a greater fullness that was previously beyond our capacity to bear. We *atone* as our new, more capacious self becomes one with all previous selves and worlds that have given rise to this new embodied moment. Every act of atonement is a new creation, infinitely.

In short, we are invited to enjoy however much Divine Reality we are willing to receive (see Doctrine and Covenants 88:32). We have the opportunity to *fall up* from one stage of maturity into a fuller embodiment, a greater Majesty, without end.

To the extent that we allow our hearts to be softened and our souls coaxed in the direction of That alone which is Good, we increase in Light and grow into the stature of what we are meant to become. I would add my personal belief to this account that there are angels cheering for us all, even now, eager for our success on this path. Our victory is their victory. An increase in Light for one is an increase in Light for all.

In a poignant moment of remembrance, Eliza Snow artfully points to what is at once our divine origin and destiny:

> Yet ofttimes a secret something
> Whispered, "You're a stranger here,"
> And I felt that I had wandered
> From a more exalted sphere.[2]

The "secret something" that whispered to Snow whispers the same *sweet everythings* in your ear too. It is Spirit calling you to remember that who you think you are is but a fleck of sea foam on the ocean's surface. Who you actually are is an Infinite Self without beginning or end.

In the next chapter, we turn our attention to the profound transformations of this Infinite Self that are available to us here and now in this very body.

DIAGRAM

Creation, Fall, Atonement

CREATION, FALL, ATONEMENT

A.

creation

fall

atonement

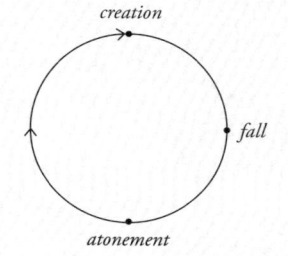

A. In traditional Christianity, our goal is to return to the presence of God. The Fall is a calamity that Christ's Atonement remedies. Our desire is to get back to where we started.

B.

B. In Latter-day Saint theology, the Fall is better understood as an ascent. Physical embodiment is a leap into a greater measure of divinity. Our desire is to continually progress on our path to godhood.

C.

D.

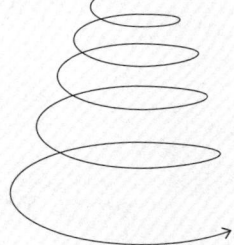

C. Restoration theology integrates a return to God's Presence with ongoing progression, giving us a spiral: endless creation, fall, and atonement (circular) through new stages of divinity (vertical growth), always in widening rings of Being. Matter becomes increasingly fine and pure.

D. Developing into godliness is not only a path of growing up—we are also learning to "grow down." On this descending path, we continually reach down and transform all that we embody and embrace with Inspiration and Love.

CREATION, FALL, ATONEMENT | 149

Chapter 6

Transformations of Faith

GOD'S ORCHESTRA

I was seven years or so into a dedicated meditation practice that had become my spiritual lifeline. Somewhere along the way, I noticed this discipline was stimulating spiritual growth in ways I didn't have language for and hadn't anticipated. I simply wasn't the same person who had started out on the path so many years ago. One of my mentors at the time was attuned to my subtle shifts and passed a book on to me. It explored the subject of developmental psychology, especially the stages of adult development, among other themes. At that point in my life, this book was, without a doubt, the most mind-altering book I had ever read.

By this time, I'd been away from any Church activity for twelve years. I had lived as much of my life out of the Church as I had in it. In some ways, my membership as a Latter-day Saint was fading into a distant memory. Then entered this book that outwardly had nothing to do with the restored gospel but would ultimately reveal an entirely new religious path to me.[1]

As I read about the stages of adult development, some of it felt very familiar, like I'd lived on that land and had worked the soil of those fields for many seasons. Other terrain the author described felt like exotic, foreign country that I could only dream of visiting one day. Somewhere in my sojourn through that text, I had a shock of recognition. The spontaneous thought came to me, "I can be Mormon again!" It came out of nowhere, and I remember thinking what a weird thing that was to think. I hadn't even realized I wanted to be "Mormon" again. But here I was, initiated into the territory of adult development, and that was what innocently came to mind. All at once, I could see how many different ways there were to live a life of authentic faith.

For example, the author emphasized how in one stage of development we tend to be more identified with tradition and collectively held values. In another stage, we become more interested in clarifying our personal values, sometimes at the expense of group belonging. Still other stages have a heightened awareness of marginalized voices and those who we tend to exclude from our circle of care. I was reading these stage descriptions and quickly realized how easily one worldview and set of values could collide with another. For the first time, I was starting to see that different styles of faith may not recognize one another as genuinely faithful.

It occurred to me, "Maybe I didn't just 'lose faith' when I was young. Maybe by no fault of my own, I ended up in a new space where I saw things just a little bit differently." That single thought changed everything. From that moment on, I no longer felt like a savage feeding on raw meat in the wilderness. I was a Latter-day Saint, a faithful one at that—and my heart longed to return to the community in worship and service.

It took me several years after this epiphany to settle back in at Church, partly because I had significant commitments to the Buddhist tradition that would take time to integrate into my newly resurrected Christian faith. But after that moment of insight, there was no going back. I could feel the power of my tradition, my lineage and ancestors flowing through me again. I sensed this path would gradually unveil for me the infinite spectrum of consciousness, the fullness of human-divinity that had always been the substance of my soul.

My Granddad Wirthlin gave a general conference talk a few years after my initial insight titled "Concern for the One," which struck a chord related to the topic of authentic faith. He spoke to the "erroneous belief that all members of the Church should look, talk, and be alike. The Lord did not people the earth with a vibrant orchestra of personalities only to value the piccolos of the world. Every instrument is precious and adds to the complex beauty of the symphony."[2]

Though I don't believe my granddad was consciously referring to the stages of adult development in his address, his intention to make room for different kinds of people and different expressions of faith was evident. For me, adult development was simply one of God's more recent revelations of just how unique each of us can be.

Such were my early impressions of adult development—another witness to God's radically inclusive Love and our unlimited capacity to grow as human-divine beings. The shift in perspective has left me permanently altered and continues to breathe new wonder into my life.

Since that time, almost twenty years ago now, I have had conversations with countless Latter-day Saints who are learning to hear their own voice and to make music that is uniquely theirs. I'm more convinced than ever that developmental models, used with humility and the Spirit's guidance, can help us love our neighbor and our God in greater measure. They can help us cohere as a faith community and make more beautiful music together in a time of great dissonance.

A BRIEF HISTORY

Human development is not a new concept. We've always known that humans grow and change. Since ancient times, we have both celebrated and facilitated the process of transformation through rituals and rites of passage. From birth to adolescence, adulthood to elderhood, up to and including the passage of death itself, the human being undergoes dramatic changes in a lifespan. Something fundamentally changed in the way we understood development in the twentieth century, though. A brilliant Swiss researcher by the name of Jean Piaget (1896–1980) brought the scientific method to bear on the process of human development, revealing an unprecedented level of detail and precision.

Piaget's central insight was that humans do not simply see the world as it is. The mind *constructs* meaning based on our *cognitive development*. Depending on our stage of cognitive development, we come to different interpretations of who we are and how the world works.

While Piaget is widely regarded as a pioneer in developmental studies, it didn't take long for other researchers to expand on his work, taking it in innovative directions. There are too many notable scientists and researchers in this field to name in this single book chapter. Still, there is one in particular who is worth mentioning briefly: James Fowler.

Steeped in a rich atmosphere of developmental studies at Harvard University back in the 1970s, Fowler is perhaps the first researcher to explicitly tie the *developmental process* to *religious experience* through rigorous empirical methods. While other developmentalists have explored applications ranging from cognition to moral development to the nature of the ego,[3] Fowler concerned himself with how we human beings make meaning in the context of faith. He demonstrated that as humans develop, the way we conceive of faith and express that faith in the world also develops. Fowler referred to this maturation process as *stages*, or *styles* of faith.

Beyond the highly valuable descriptions of the stages themselves, what we learn from Fowler's research is that in any given congregation, in any given faith tradition, there exists a broad spectrum of faith.

This matters. Without a proper understanding of the developmental process that is occurring for all of us throughout adulthood, we run the risk of dismissing certain styles of genuine faith as unfaithful. More damaging yet, the style of faith that is dominant in any given culture and tradition will naturally tend to marginalize, even vilify, other styles whose features it does not recognize. My hope is that in the descriptions that follow, you can come to a greater sense of reverence and awe for the diversity of faith that Sacred Reality raises up from the very stones, in your life and in mine (see Matthew 3:9).

A SIMPLE DEVELOPMENTAL MAP

To describe some of the features and terrain of human development, I want to offer a map. Good maps give us the information we need and ignore the rest. If I'm in Zion National Park, a map that tells me the chemical composition of the red rock or how many tens of millions of years old the different strata are may be fascinating. But ultimately, that map won't be useful to me if I'm just looking for a place to have a two-egg breakfast in town.

In the following sections, I'm going to offer a high-level view of how consciousness—Light—develops and evolves *as* the human-divine being. I will dedicate more space to the most common stages, but I will also include meaningful detail on some of the statistically rare stages. My hope is to include just enough information to help you start to grasp the vital importance of this cartography. The primary language I'll use to demarcate what I've been calling stages and styles up until now is that of *person perspectives*. This framework is an innovation and major contribution to our understanding of human development that comes from the scholar-practitioner Dr. Susanne Cook-Greuter.

What is a person perspective? *Person perspective* refers specifically to how many distinct viewpoints or perspectives we can integrate in our meaning-making. Put more plainly, a person perspective describes how we know ourselves, others, and the world around us. At times, I'll also use other words to point to this process. For example, "stages" is probably the most common metaphor for describing human development.

My issue with "stages" is that it emphasizes a linear, sequential movement from earlier to later stages. While sequential growth is important—for example, we all had to learn to walk before we could run—it creates an unwelcome illusion that later stages are somehow inherently better or more advanced than the earlier stages. Development is in fact omnidirectional—we grow up, we grow down, we grow all around. We revisit previous spaces with new awareness, and the most foundational of our developmental qualities are each God seeds in their own right.

For this reason, I'll use terms such as *qualities, virtues, worldviews,* and *meaning-making strategies* to shake us out of our stubborn Western habit of imposing rigid hierarchies over *everything*. The context will make clear what I'm pointing to. Rather than bandy more abstractions about, let's start with a zero-person perspective and work our way up to get a feel for how the person perspectives unfold.

ZERO-PERSON PERSPECTIVE

At the zero-person perspective, we have not yet formed an inward image of "self," and therefore, by definition, there are zero persons in this perspective.[4] This is the domain of the human in utero and the newborn child, who has not yet reached a level of maturity where a self has separated out from the undifferentiated flow of reality. There is no experience of "inside" or "outside," no experience of experience at all—only the vibrating, crackling activity of a cosmos that does not yet know itself. In this perspective, we are one with the Ground of Being.

It may not seem like there's much more to explore here. In fact, words cannot begin to describe the fertile *Field* of potential that constitutes this foundational pre-perspective. Spiritual adepts from across the ages have described experiences that seem to clearly point to this stratum of consciousness, specifically how we can learn to return to it and draw from its Power. Zen Buddhists have used terms such as *zero* and *beginner's mind* to gesture toward this profound meditative realization. Christian mystics invoke the "Groundless Ground" and "Dazzling Dark" to point to the intimacy of Divine Union. Even modern neuroscience suggests that there is a way in which prayer and meditation can help us access different levels of mind and therefore recover the experiential richness that is lost the moment we start to form a sense of separate self.[5]

This segues into a pattern I want to sensitize you to early on. When we move beyond the zero-person perspective, we enfold it in our development as we grow up. That is, as we begin to construct the first-person perspective, the zero-person perspective remains available to us. It is "nested" in our being, forming the foundational layer of who we're becoming. We can learn to return to earlier perspectives in our development throughout life, bringing new maturity and depth to them as we do so. Paradoxically, this ability implies that the so-called early perspectives house some of our most mature capacities simultaneously.[6] The question in human-divine development then becomes the following: How do we fully embody and refine the gifts that are uniquely ours to cultivate?[7]

FIRST-PERSON PERSPECTIVE

Margaret Mahler and her colleagues assert that in the age range of about four to five months, the transition from zero-person perspective into early first-person perspective occurs, a period of time they call "hatching" or psychological birth.[8] Barring mental disability, traumatic brain injury, and illness-induced vegetative states, we all develop out of the zero-person perspective effortlessly within the first year of life.

In this first year, an inchoate mental model of the separation between "I" and world begins to take shape. We are on our way to becoming a self, one that is differentiated from the physical world—at least to an extent. And with a self, specifically a locus of perception, comes perspective. As the etymology suggests—*per-specere*—we start to *look through* the lens of a proto-self.

First-person perspective means that we can only take one person's perspective—our own. This is the stage of "I, me, mine." Psychologists sometimes call this range of development "egocentric," not in a pejorative sense but in a purely descriptive one. The "ego" is at the center of the world. There are other beings and agents in this world, but we haven't yet developed the complexity of consciousness to realize that. As far as we know, we're wandering around in an empty world, following only our own impulses.

Imagine you're sitting in a sandbox and you see a toy that irresistibly draws you in. You literally can't imagine that the child playing with the toy will feel sad if you steal it. There is, in fact, no such thing as stealing at the first-person perspective. I'm the only "person" I'm aware of. And by person, in this case, I mean a throbbing, pulsing field of life force constantly seeking gratification. I want that, I take it. I'm hungry, I eat it. It gets in my way, I yell at it. Developmentalists have also called this the "impulsive stage" for obvious reasons!

Lest you suppose this perspective is very distant from you and far in your past, think back to the last time you got overly hungry, sleepy, or caught in some bad weather. It was probably difficult to escape your foul mood until your basic needs were taken care of. If you feel someone getting in your way—such as an intimate partner disagreeing with your point of view, a friend failing to consider your feelings—try to appreciate how quickly your capacity to take another person's point of view collapses into survival mode. Recall the previous chapter on the energy centers. Essentially, every time we (almost always irrationally) feel as though our survival is at stake, we instinctively drop into a first-person perspective where we feel we can adequately defend ourselves. "It's me against the world!" Most of us do this much more often than we realize, whether subtly or overtly. It's not all bad news at this stage, though.

Gifts of the First-Person Perspective

One of the profound gifts of the first-person perspective is the coming into our own personal power. In the earliest days of life, we swim around in that oh-so-soothing oceanic feeling. But after a while, we all figured out that with these arms and legs, we can move around in the world. We can explore things. We discover our own desire and that we have agency. We learn that we can do what we want, and we can express our desire in the world. There's a tremendous amount of life force in the first-person perspective as it matures.

I have a funny story that illustrates this developmental quality. My wife and I were staying with some family in Portland a few years ago when my nephew Miles was exploring the far reaches of power in the first-person perspective. Not yet parents at that time, we hadn't been fully initiated into the realities of raising a little one.

We were staying across the hall from him in the guest room when we both awoke to a blood-curdling scream at 6:00 a.m.: "I! WANT! SCREEN TIME! I! WANT! SCREEN TIME!" The only break Miles took was to gasp for more air on the inbreath. His voice rattled the walls and stung my nerves for a solid thirty minutes. At first I was predictably irritated. But after several minutes, my irritation gave way to wonder, in spite of myself. The sheer vitality of a child's raw, unabashed desire—I could only marvel at his stamina.

As adults, it's all too easy to lose touch with our vitality. It's seductively easy to forget what we really want in life. I don't mean to romanticize this perspective. I'm not suggesting as adults we need to take other people's stuff and scream at the top of our lungs every time we don't get what we want. Impulse control comes next in our developmental journey, and it's a welcome upgrade.

What I am suggesting is that with healthy development, we always have the opportunity to bring our higher awareness to the qualities that emerged earlier in our development. Life force is as foundational a quality as there is in human life. But have we learned to remain fully open to the great gift of Life and draw from the Divine Energy of which we are a unique expression? To paraphrase Picasso, we are all born vital. The task is to remain vital as we grow up into the fullness of Divinity.

EXERCISE: CONNECTING WITH LIFE FORCE

If you're feeling adventurous, you can go somewhere you feel safe, then unleash your inner two-year-old and say as loud as you like: "I! WANT! _____!" Whatever it is, just let it come from deep in the belly, from the marrow of your bones. This exercise will get you in touch with the life force pretty quickly.

The more subtle version of this exercise is to take a journal and start with the following sentence stem: "What I really want is . . ." Complete that sentence and just see where it takes you. You can write the sentence stem again and again, completing it in a different way each time (e.g., "What I really want is . . . to quit my job and move to Italy." "What I really want is . . . to have deeper intimacy with my partner."). Or you can just write an extended entry on a single thing that you really want.

For example, "What I really want is . . . to eat good food with friends and share stories of how challenging life can be." If I were journaling, I would just follow that impulse and see where it takes me. As you journal, I encourage you to let your hand keep moving. Try not to censor. Notice the voice of the censor coming up, let it be present, but let it be in the background. These pages aren't for anyone else to see. You can dispose of them any way you wish when you're done writing.

As adults, we censor and limit our own vitality. We're afraid of what we want because we've learned from an early age that what we want can be dangerous. But we're not talking about acting anything out. Not yet. This exercise is just to tap into the raw, primordial life force that animates and quickens you. Later on we can work on refining and honing our wants and desires appropriately in service of the entire body of Christ.

JOURNAL EXERCISE:

Sentence stem: What I really want is . . .

Be honest. Don't censor. Keep your hand moving. Burn the paper you write on when you're done if you have to. Feel the life force waking up in your body and let it blaze.

TRANSFORMATIONS OF FAITH | 161

SECOND-PERSON PERSPECTIVE

In the second-person perspective, we grow out of our egocentrism into "sociocentrism." Recall that by "egocentrism," psychologists are not making a value judgment that someone is selfish or brutish or difficult to be around (though that may be true for some individuals). Psychologists are describing the person's ego complexity.

Sociocentric implies that our identity is now held in "society." That is, we understand who we are by way of our relationships. This perspective is all about relating with others. At the level of cognitive development, we're forming a more mature *theory of mind*, which refers to our ability to attribute mind states (e.g., intentions, hopes, expectations, motivations, desires, beliefs) to others and thereby make sense of their actions. In other words, we no longer experience ourselves to be the sole inhabitant of the universe. The interiority, the subjectivity of *the other* slowly dawns in our consciousness. We see that other people have feelings and desires just like we do and that they matter.[9]

Gifts of the Second-Person Perspective

Second-person perspective is the great shift from "I" to "we." I can actually see you for the first time—at least, gradually. You are different from me, and together we form a we. Your wants matter just like my wants matter, and so the negotiating begins. From this perspective, we have to learn to start sharing with others and getting along. Over time we learn what it means to be in a family with others, in a church, in a community. To do this, we make agreements with each other. We make rules that follow a basic logic: "I'm not going to do this to you because I would hate it if you did this to me." Sound familiar? From a psychological point of view, the Golden Rule becomes possible from a second-person perspective. From the first-person perspective, might makes right: we want it, we take it. But society is simply not functional if everyone follows this "I-me-mine" logic. Human relationship breaks down when everybody is simply looking out for themselves.

A monumental shift occurs as our minds become capable of constructing the experience of *other*. From a second-person perspective, we realize we can do more as a collective than we can as individuals if we learn to cooperate. One of the guiding questions of this meaning-making strategy[10] then becomes the following: How are we going to get along? If I protect your needs and trust you to protect mine, we can establish order and harmony in our *shared* world. We only need to establish the rules and to follow them.

When there is good alignment in this range of development, we feel steady affection from our family, our loved ones, from whoever our ingroup happens to be. We feel safety in belonging. Not only that, but belonging to a particular family, tribe, and tradition, we share a common story of transcendent value and purpose. We develop divine confidence in who we are, where we're from, and what we're here to do.

If I start to feel lost in life, I can orient to tradition: What did my ancestors do to overcome similar adversity a hundred years ago? How is this trial a part of God's plan for us? Prior to this perspective, the meaning of life is more immediate. It's all about satisfying my raw desires. Life from the second-person perspective is more community- and story-based. I learn to subordinate my impulses in pursuit of a collective purpose. I draw meaning and purpose from stories that connect me to the most important people in my life. As Latter-day Saints, some of our highest, shared purposes include becoming more like Christ and building a Zion community. These examples are yet another instance where a seemingly early and unsophisticated stage of development bears within it the seeds of Infinity.

Pitfalls of the Second-Person Perspective

While the capacity to identify with others is the great developmental achievement of the second-person perspective, it can quickly become the primary pitfall. That is, we have a tendency here to overidentify with our ingroup. In practice, *overidentify* means we are inclined to believe in an unexamined way that the group we identify with—our church, our nation—is inherently better than others. When our ingroup comes under criticism, we easily justify our behavior and struggle to imagine that we're capable of wrongdoing. From a religious perspective, we might say, "We're on *God's side* after all. 'Those people' are on the *other* side."

The liabilities of this perspective are even more insidious than the tendency to overidentify with our tribe. Not only do we have a hard time seeing our own shortcomings here, but we are also prone to projecting our negative qualities onto others. *Projection* refers to the way we attribute qualities to others that we would prefer not to see in ourselves. Jesus cuts through this tribal egotism when he commands us to "first get rid of the log in your own eye; then you will see well enough to deal with the speck in your friend's eye" (Matthew 7:5, NLT).

A practice I've worked with regarding this particular stumbling block is as follows: Any time I find myself fixating on the shortcomings of another person or group, I first try and catch myself in the act. Then I notice if I have access to compassionate understanding. Is my intention to empathize with them in their weakness and see if I might offer something needed, or am I secretly getting a thrill by imagining that I am superior to them in some way?

If I don't feel compassion in my heart towards the other, I'm immediately skeptical of where I'm coming from. I become skeptical of my own motivations. When I'm willing to look, I realize I'm avoiding seeing something even more vulnerable in myself.

I remember being with a group of young Latter-day Saints on my first visit to China and going to see a Buddhist temple. A number of them commented that they couldn't feel the Spirit there. They said the space felt "pagan" and "dark." Being an estranged member of the Church and a practicing Buddhist at that time, I felt hurt by the comments. It wasn't until many years later I was able to articulate that those young students were *projecting* their own qualities onto that temple. At a deeper level, what I believe they were saying was something like, "I don't know how to feel the Spirit when I'm outside of my own religious comfort zone."

We enter the very beginnings of the second-person perspective anywhere from around age four to six, after which the temptation to create "us versus them" dynamics stays with us the rest of our lives. On the other hand, the sacred sense of belonging and higher purpose we draw from our companions and communities are qualities we can magnify and share generously throughout our lives. As with every developmental revelation, these potentials are what we make of them.

Holy Envy

A great practice you can do to protect yourself against the potential liabilities of the second-person perspective is that of "holy envy." What is holy envy? A term originally coined by Krister Stendahl, former bishop of the Church of Sweden, it essentially means to leave room to admire all the sacred qualities in faith traditions that are not your own. I had an intense experience with holy envy long before I learned this helpful term.

I was a foreign student in China when I met members of the Baha'i faith for the first time. One thing that especially struck me as I spent more time around my new friends was that they were highly conscientious about backbiting. The first time I consciously noticed this, I was complaining about someone in our small expat community when my Baha'i friend looked at me and said matter-of-factly, "That's backbiting." I remember feeling dazed, like she'd poked me right between the eyes when she said it. Her energy, crisp and clear, communicated to me in no uncertain terms, "Don't do that. It's hurtful." After I met other people in the Baha'i faith, I noticed that they had a similar practice around not speaking ill of others, especially those who were not present.

I felt the power and integrity of this practice, so thought I would give it a go. Every time I was tempted to say something unkind or caught myself in the act of saying something unkind about somebody who wasn't present, I asked myself, "Why am I doing that?" Almost always I found it was to avoid a deeper vulnerability I was feeling. Either I felt threatened by that person, or their negative qualities reminded me way too much of my own.

Years later, I came home from China and found a description of a teacher's duty in the Doctrine and Covenants: "To watch over the church always, and be with and strengthen them. And see that there is no iniquity in the church, neither hardness with each other, neither lying, backbiting, nor evil speaking" (Doctrine and Covenants 20:53–54).

There it was in plain English: no backbiting. I realized we had also received revelation around this principle, but we hadn't learned to radiate the power of this teaching as the Baha'i faith had done.

This isn't the only quality I admire in the Baha'i people. But I offer it as an example of holy envy. I envy the Baha'i people for how meticulously they take care of one another by not saying hurtful things behind one another's backs.

The practice of holy envy leads to acknowledging the genuine spiritual gifts in other traditions, and it calls us to be better at living the fullness of our own tradition. It even helps us to see that our tradition cannot realize its fullness without the gifts of other traditions to teach and inspire us along the way.

HOLY ENVY:

Think of the faith traditions present in your circle of friends, community, and country. Write about at least one quality they have that you admire, that you seek to emulate.

JOURNAL EXERCISE:

Ask yourself the question: Am I overidentified with the specialness of my family? With the "trueness" of my church? The superiority of my political party? My country? Be honest. Challenge yourself. Consider asking a trusted friend or mentor to engage in a reflective conversation about these questions with you.

THIRD-PERSON PERSPECTIVE

The third-person perspective in many ways is synonymous with objectivity. Our perceptions are now less susceptible to the sway of individual impulses and cultural influences. We can stand back, to a degree, and observe experience in a relatively more detached way. Many Western institutions are designed to form human beings in this particular strategy of meaning-making. As a result, this perspective is in the air we breathe and the water we drink. It is the dominant way of knowing in the modern world.

Questions like "Why is the sky blue?" can come up quite early in life. But at the third-person perspective, our capacity to analyze, reason, and understand becomes more powerful. "Why is the sky blue?" becomes more like "How does the chemical composition of the elements in the atmosphere appear to the human eye as this particular hue?" Questions become more penetrating and touch on more complex cause-and-effect relationships.[11]

At the third-person perspective, we "back off" from the second-person perspective of shared group meaning. The worldview we formed from the second-person perspective now becomes visible to us as a new object of inquiry. This separation gives rise to a new sensibility: Is what I've always believed really true? As a result, we become more empirical in nature, questioning many of the things we've long taken for granted. Can I prove that what I believe is true? Would a neutral observer come to the same conclusions I have given the evidence? At the second-person perspective, our instinct is to appeal to shared stories and cultural authority figures: our leaders say this is true, so it's true. Now at the third-person perspective, a new burden of proof appears.

The third-person perspective is the first we have looked at thus far that does not emerge for all adults. Though comprehensive cross-cultural studies have yet to be conducted, we know that there is a significant number of adults who occupy the second-person perspective throughout life. If the third-person perspective does emerge, my experience is that it tends to do so around late adolescence into the early twenties at the very earliest.

Gifts of the Third-Person Perspective
Technologies

This tectonic shift in human consciousness has changed the face of human culture and the earth itself since the dawn of the modern period. Newly preoccupied with empirical data and how the world objectively works, humans have developed technologies that would have been inconceivable even one hundred years ago. From enhanced food production to modern medicine, climate-controlled housing to clean energy, the human mind has an astonishing capacity to discern the laws of nature and cooperate with them in a way that improves quality of life.

This capacity in our development not only applies to technological systems but also human systems. How we choose to govern ourselves has changed dramatically with the advent of the third-person perspective. For example, I grew up under a constitutional democracy in the United States. One of the basic premises of a democracy is that each citizen can obtain information about the candidates that hope to represent them. Based on objective information and my own personal values, I can cast a vote for my candidate of choice. If each citizen casts a vote for their preferred candidate in this way, then over time, more people will be represented by candidates who are responsive to their preferences.

Examples abound in this space. But what I want to illustrate is that different person perspectives open up new possibilities not available to prior ones. It is not until the third-person perspective that we start to conceive of ourselves (and others) as autonomous subjects with the choice to pursue individual ideals.

Self as Object of Investigation

Not only do we see the world from this perspective, we can turn this perspective in on ourselves, at which point the self becomes an empirical object of investigation. "As without, so within," it reads in the Emerald Tablet, a text used by European and Islamic alchemists. In other words, as I see the outside world more objectively, I start to objectify the self. Puzzling over the inner world newly available to consciousness, I try to get at the truth of the matter—who am I, really?

Again, we can ask the question "Who am I?" at earlier stages of development. But in the third-person perspective, the question takes on a new quality: Am I really living in alignment with my values? I say

I believe one thing, but then I do another. Why is that? There must be a deeper truth I'm not aware of. In this perspective, I can now look at my life in terms of discrete categories—past, present, and future. What shaped me when I was young? Who am I now? And who can I become? From a second-person perspective, we are preoccupied with rules and roles. The path is well-defined—we need only to follow it. At the third-person perspective, however, our unique personhood moves to the foreground. I ask myself, How can I become the best version of *myself* possible? This question implies that I will have to walk a new path—one that no one else has ever walked before.

A reckoning with the self comes at this stage. Do I really agree with what my family taught me to value? Do I agree with what I learned to value at church? In society? Are any of these ideas actually mine or did I just pick them up from my environment? Until now, we've been like a fish in water, not realizing that water is wet. The good news is that swimming in the waters of our cultures and traditions, we drink in the gifts and virtues that flow through them. The bad news is that to whatever extent our community has unexamined prejudices, or what Joseph Campbell aptly calls "sanctified misunderstanding,"[12] we tend to swallow that too.

At a certain point, if we wish to mature, we have to stand on our own two feet. We get to decide for ourselves what we want. Therefore, it becomes very important at this stage of development to discern, What do I actually value? Forget everyone else. What do I choose for my life?

From Commandment to Commitment
There's a phrase I like to use to describe the developmental shift that occurs at the third-person perspective: from commandments to commitments.

Recall from the first-person perspective, there really are no rules. Or rather, there are rules going on in parallel to our egocentric world, but we are blissfully unaware of them. At the second-person perspective, we learn to play nice. We share our favorite toy with a friend, trusting that the same behavior will come back around and benefit us in time. We learn to fold our arms in the chapel and love to be praised for following the rules so perfectly. We learn the goodness of belonging.

With belonging comes rules. We won't belong to a community for long if we can't respect and observe its basic practices. In Judeo-Christian parlance, we often call these commandments. For a certain period in life (from roughly four years old through adolescence), commandments are preeminent and developmentally appropriate. We're still learning to tame the body's appetites and to live in a stark world of right and wrong. Commandments offer a concrete, "growthful" structure that maximizes our potential to flourish.

There comes a time, however, when tonic becomes toxin. What was life and growth yesterday may be death and servitude today. If we continue to relate to the commandments as an outside force imposing its will on us, we will miss the developmental opportunity to shift our locus of control and authority from external to internal. We will fail to develop true self-reliance. Brigham Young understood this developmental pitfall intuitively: "I am more afraid that this people have so much confidence in their leaders that they will not inquire for themselves of God whether they are led by Him. I am fearful they settle down in a state of blind self-security, trusting their eternal destiny in the hands of their leaders with a reckless confidence that in itself would thwart the purposes of God in their salvation, and weaken that influence they could give to their leaders, did they know for themselves, by the revelations of Jesus, that they are led in the right way."[13]

To obey leaders in a state of "blind self-security . . . would thwart the purposes of God in [our] salvation." President Young implies that God's purpose is to grow us into autonomous beings capable of discerning for ourselves what is good. If we outsource this process of discernment to another, we will never exercise our divine capacity to choose for ourselves. It's not about being commanded anymore. We know the commandments by heart. But knowing something by heart and a change of heart are two very different realities.

What Christ wants is to change the substance of our beings. Anyone can go with the flow, following the rules in order to blend with the masses. Following rules alone does not forge us into celestial beings. At the third-person perspective, a new question stares us in the face: What do I commit myself to? As a psychologically emancipated person, what do I choose to do with this *terrible freedom*? *Terrible* because we are now ultimately responsible for our own destiny. We're on the hook for the good and bad decisions alike. Shifting from commandment-following to commitment-making agents, we show God and the heavens the stuff we're made of.

Developmentally we get a bit of a free ride through the second-person perspective: the mama bird delivers our meals to us prechewed. At the third-person perspective, however, growth becomes more effortful and deliberate, like a subtle pioneer trek across the uncharted plains of soul and psyche.

In summary, when I construct a third-person perspective, I become the author of my own life. Irrespective of the family, community, and culture that raised me, I start to discern what is right for *me*, a unique person, even if my choices fly in the face of conventional wisdom. Even as those who insist that I conform to group norms clutch at my ankles and beg me to stay with the horde, I must strike out into the world to offer what I alone can offer.

Pitfalls of Third-Person Perspective

Strengths are often our weaknesses. One of our strengths at the third-person perspective is the *power to become*. I can imagine a more beautiful version of myself that I know in my heart to be possible, and

I plan to pursue it with integrity and tenacity until one day, I have lived into that possibility and made it real.

It's difficult for us to see from this perspective that *being* is the complementary quality of *becoming*. Without a healthy grounding in being, our becoming can feel ragged and depleted. Our strong tendency here is to chase after what we might become some far-off day at the expense of connecting to our *inherent Wholeness* right now. In this way, life from a third-person perspective can become a never-ending self-improvement project.

Because I have the sophistication now to look inward and ask whether I am the person I'm supposed to be, I also have the sophistication to pursue future possibilities at the expense of the present. We can and often do exhaust ourselves in this space of development. No matter how much we accomplish, it can feel like it's never enough. We can easily start to feel like "*I'm* never enough." In religious life, the feeling of not being enough readily translates into a sense of unworthiness.

Related to compulsive self-improvement is the sense of isolation that can come from having an authentic self to improve in the first place. Ironically, the crystallization of an individuated identity leaves us more vulnerable to feeling estranged from others and from God. Too much individuality can easily lead to not enough communion, not enough sustaining relationship. As powerful as the gifts of this stage are, they bring with them a concomitant risk of loneliness and despair. We are more prone to feeling alone here than anywhere else in our developmental journey.

Another simultaneous strength and stumbling block in this territory is what can become an obsession with *intellectual knowledge*. It's not surprising that precisely as we become more cognitively capable of investigating the self and world, we may develop a fixation on knowing the absolute truth of things. There is a strong tendency to intellectualize everything from this perspective. The harmful version of this need-to-know perspective in gospel life is two-pronged: we might deny the experience of not-knowing or disparage nonrational modes of knowing.

When we deny the experience of not knowing, we pretend to be more certain about elements of our faith than we actually are, always ready to rationalize and defend every last doctrinal point. It wounds our cerebral pride at this stage to imagine that there are not only things we don't know but *can't know*. One antidote to this trap is to practice relaxing into *unknowing* at appropriate times, learning to tolerate the anxiety we feel when we don't have all the answers.

The other risk in this perspective is that we may reject other modes of knowing all together in favor of scientific, empirical knowledge. This intellectual tyranny can stymie our progress to the extent that we're unwilling to be touched and transformed by the spirit through all of our faculties, not just the thinking mind. I detailed the antidote to this temptation in chapter two—honoring sacred embodiment at all levels.

REFLECTIVE JOURNALING:

A classic construct that originates from the third-person perspective is the "Five-Year Plan."

Based on what you value and what you commit yourself to, where do you want to be five years from now? What do you want your life to look like?

What smaller goals might you set for yourself to make sure you stay on track with the bigger five-year plan?

Take some time to flesh out the details. Appreciate the way you're able to imagine possible futures and work towards the one you find to be most worthy. This ability is just a taste of the many gifts that flow from this bandwidth of development.

MEDITATION
Perfect and Progressing

THE RHYTHM OF DEVELOPMENT

Having moved through a few different perspectives now, I hope you're beginning to feel the rhythm in your bones: at each unique perspective, we back off from the previous perspective that used to feel like "me," and we realize there's a new someone looking at the old me. Dr. Robert Kegan famously described development in terms of this subject/object dynamic: "Growth always involves a process of differentiation, of emergence from embeddedness, thus creating out of the former subject a new object to be taken by the new subjectivity."[14]

The subject is who we take ourselves to be; the subject is our felt sense of self. We can't see it, question it, or examine its assumptions any more than an eyeball can turn around and see itself. It's the view we're looking *from*. From our particular view (what we've been calling *person perspectives*), certain "objects" come into view. Objects are what we, the subject, can be aware of. The whole science and art of development describes the way in which, somehow, what we previously took to be subject comes into view as an object. We see the subject now, which by definition, makes it an object. The question becomes, who is this new subject seeing the previous subject? Herein lies the mystery. Our capacity to embody new subjectivity, as if born again to a greater measure of Life, Love, and Light, seems to be unending.

Development in this sense is a continual falling back from a perspective that once gave coherence to our sense of self, other, and world. As soon as our perspective shifts, a new view of self, other, and world reveals itself. What's distinct about the fourth-person perspective (which we're about to explore), especially in the more mature and later ranges of this territory, is that for the first time, we start to consciously realize that this whole subject/object movement is happening. We realize that throughout our whole lives, we've been moving from one sense of self to the next. Therefore, in this range of development, we can start to appreciate that *this self too* is just another temporary constellation of perspectives, surely with broader, more beautiful vistas on the horizon.

One of the mysteries of human development is that certain people will gravitate to a particular meaning-making strategy and make it their station in life. In other words, although stages and perspectives seem to be unending, we don't all feel called to grow vertically in the same way. By vertical growth, I'm referring to the sequential unfolding of person perspectives—from zero-person through sixth-person perspective (and who knows what lies beyond that in the eternities). I mentioned above that a significant number of adults reside in the second-person perspective as a homebase and draw their sense of meaning, purpose, and identity from there. Others will take up residence in the third-person perspective and find no end to the gifts, challenges, and opportunities it affords.

And yet for some people, for reasons that we don't entirely understand, the third-person perspective will wear out. With the old garment now threadbare, these wanderers put on new clothes to cover themselves on the next stage of the journey.

DIAGRAM

Person Perspectives

PERSON PERSPECTIVES

Primary Sense of Identity

Object in Awareness

Sense of self / other not clearly formed

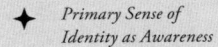

Primary Sense of Identity as Awareness

Note: *.0 represents the early expression of a person perspective while .5 represents the late expression of a person perspective.*

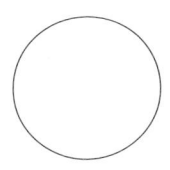

0.0
We remain undifferentiated from our Spiritual Source. Here, there is infinitely rich Divine Potential as well as Perfection.

1.0
The sacred, earthly self is born, though our sense of self is just beginning to form. We learn to get our basic needs met and to trust the goodness of Life itself.

1.5
Our sense of a physical self becomes more substantial while a sense of "other" still remains inchoate. We learn to express personal power and will.

"Our capacity to embody new subjectivity, as if born again to a greater measure of Life, Love, and Light, seems to be unending."

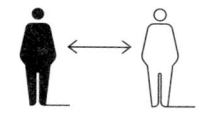

2.0
The social self is born—relationship becomes our primary sense of identity and worth. We learn to be in exchange with sacred others, to give and to receive.

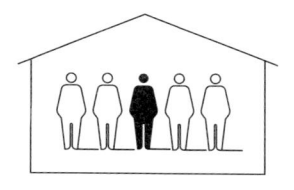

2.5
We become more adept at following rules and inhabiting roles. We are one with the sacred purpose of our collective.

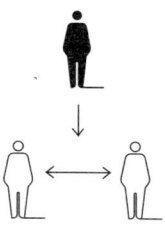

3.0
The psychologically independent self is born. We begin to step back from the holding environment of our family and culture to discern our personal values.

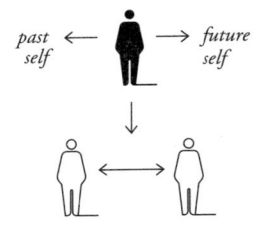

3.5

The experience of being a separate individual peaks. We reflect on who we've been, who we are, and who we might yet become.

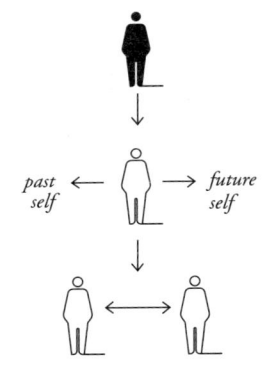

4.0

A context-aware self is born. We step back from what seemed like pure objectivity and begin seeing all the contexts that interconnect in a vast, sacred ecology.

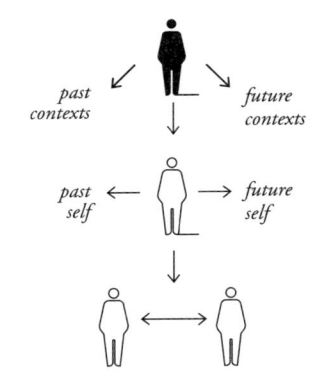

4.5

We come to see contexts as nested systems. Some perspectives are truer than others, though all perspectives have their truth, wisdom, and function.

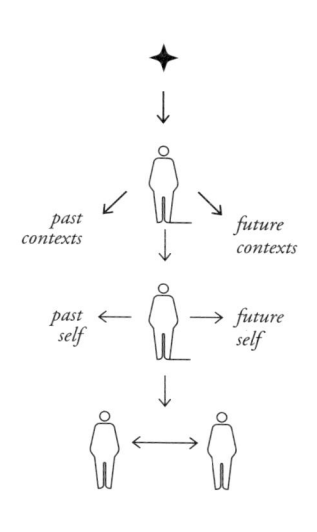

5.0
A self of pure awareness is born. We begin to witness the endless perspectives the body-mind generates and to see the open-ended nature of Reality.

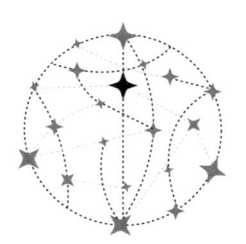

5.5
Our capacity to organize mental constructs matures. Based on our talents and passions, we engage across seemingly unrelated systems and create combinations never before seen.

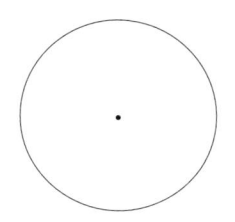

6.0+
"Self" is experienced as both Uniquely Personal and Universally Divine—Reality is One. Life, Love, and Light evolve across the eons, even as the Sacred is prior to time and space.

FOURTH-PERSON PERSPECTIVE

The activity of analyzing the self, setting goals, and always striving to become better than we were yesterday can all start to feel hollow. We come to ask, who is this person who's constantly trying to get somewhere? What if I quit trying so hard to make things happen and let things happen instead?

Here, we fall behind the third-person perspective, which we were so confident was objective and true. Now, we start to realize that no matter where we stand, we're always taking a perspective from *somewhere*. Depending on that somewhere, we will see things in a particular way, emphasizing this and deemphasizing that. In fact, reality is so vast, we can't ever possibly master the truth. If hard-nosed objectivity is the central concern at the previous stage, then it is the way subjectivity "dances" with objectivity that enters our awareness now. Subject and object are forever intertwined.

In a sea of experience, we can never master all the data, all knowledge. We can only perceive a little sliver of it. Where we were born, our biological sex, our gender, whether we're old or young, whether we speak English or Mandarin, all of these different contexts and more shape the way we make meaning of "objective" reality. Expressed in another way, all knowledge is contextual—we know what we know from a particular point of view—and contexts are infinite. The myth of pure objectivity crumbles. We see clearly that there's no such thing as a view from nowhere.

Gifts of the Fourth-Person Perspective

The fourth-person perspective is a realm of pluralism and paradox. Because we prefer to take multiple perspectives more fluidly in this range of development, we're more aware than ever that seemingly contradictory views might actually reconcile with one another at a deeper level.

To give an example, I'm in the interesting situation of being a Latter-day Saint from birth, but much of my spiritual formation came through Buddhism over the last twenty-five years. Buddhism is said to be a *nontheistic* tradition (which is much different than *atheistic*, the assertion that God does not exist), and people in the Church often ask me, "How can the restored gospel and Buddhism possibly be reconciled with such different stances on God?" In my personal experience, Latter-day Saints emphasize the aspects of God which we can know, and Buddhists tend to emphasize what we can't know about Ultimate Reality (technically known as *negative theology* in the Christian tradition). I've actually found that the Buddhist approach to spiritual life has deepened my intimacy with God immensely. Just as a fungal network breaks down organic matter, creating nutrient-rich soil to support new life, the practice of not-knowing in Buddhism mulches beliefs that have outworn their usefulness, giving rise to fresh and vibrant insights into Divine Reality.

Recall in chapter two, I wrote at some length about different ways of knowing—body, heart, mind. From a fourth-person perspective, we realize that these distinct ways of knowing are just different contexts that shape moment to moment experience—they are different flavors of Divine Life to be savored. When I visit Walden Pond on a warm summer day, I can sit on the shore and labor over Thoreau's philosophical musings one line at a time. I can open my heart to the spirit of an authentic American identity that was birthed in that geography, or I can strip down to my trunks and plunge into the cool, clear water. But even better, I can do all three. Why limit myself to only a single way of knowing when the world is so wide and vast?

A friend of mine who recently passed away was a prolific artist. Kaaren often wore pigtail braids shot through with the gray hair of a sage who had embraced the organic process of aging. Her features were smooth and round, almost elvish. Her eyes twinkled with presence when she looked at you, and she never lost her lilting Irish accent even after spending many years in the United States. Whenever I was around Kaaren, I felt sprinkled by magic fairy dust. I was transported to another realm where forests are enchanted, satyrs play their lutes, and wood nymphs flit about. There was always more time for good food, song, and matters of the heart.

She raised a beautiful family in the Church with unusually talented children who span the entire spectrum of faith and belief, some more traditional and some much less so. While some parents may have found the situation troubling, Kaaren always struck me as being appreciatively inquisitive with all of her children in their uniqueness. Rather than wag a doctrinaire finger at others for deviating from the one path, it was as if her whole being conveyed the message, "Tell me what it's like to be you." She didn't presume to know the way people *should be* so much as she let others teach her what kind of diversity was possible in human life. Her open heart didn't arbitrarily stop at the borders of her family, either. She was radiant towards me and my wife, towards other people in her neighborhood—I imagine towards everyone. Kaaren genuinely relished others' beingness and the unique perspectives that make all of us who we are.

It reminds me a bit of my experience being married to a Korean American Latter-day Saint who is also an artist. Gloria is effortlessly attuned to the aesthetic dimension of life. She knows the Sacred through color and form, through light and contrast. When she speaks, she often speaks with the same rhythm that causes the surf to lap up on the shores and the stars to wheel through the sky. She wields a gentle power like a silently flowing river—a quality I never experienced growing up in American culture. And she reminds me continually how powerful a few choice words can be when spoken from an undefended heart.

At the fourth-person perspective, we realize how utterly limited we are in our capacity to take perspectives. From the moment we're born, we're born into a way of seeing that necessarily divides up the Whole. But when we vulnerably open to another human being's experience, we can taste the magic of seeing the world through new eyes. We can recover more of our inherent complexity, literally be made more whole and holy by letting new perspectives shape our minds and hearts.

At the third-person perspective, we take ourselves to be an individual who is on their way to somewhere important. This view is partially true. Entering the fourth-person perspective, we start to relax more into the moment, letting experience wash over us. We like to feel things change moment to moment and to move with the flux. At one point, we strived to know who we were. Now, we let the present moment reveal new aspects of ourselves to us in a kaleidoscopic flow.

We realize that we cannot be whole without one another's unique embodiments. I recover more of my innate complexity, more of the fullness of being by appreciating the way you live out the fullness of your being. And so we love to be in the fullness and the resonance of community at this stage. The notion that there are absolute truths that we must cleave to softens. Notice how I say "softens." Truth doesn't go away. (Where could it go?!) We still very much respond to Truth in this new walk of life. But our naïve belief that we had mastered the truth, that *this is what we call it* and *this is how we do it*, all of that starts to soften. We realize that Truth bodies forth innumerable forms. Through a plurality of perspectives, we learn more about the Fullness and the Wholeness of Truth than we ever could by nailing it down, by pinning the butterfly's wings. In my own life, it was through the Mind of the Buddha that I was broken open by the Heart of Christ, revealing to me in an instant that truly everything flows into and through everything else.

Pitfalls of the Fourth-Person Perspective

In this new space, we are less goal-oriented than the third-person perspective and more process-oriented. We learn to relax into the present moment and to become more of a mystery to ourselves in a way that is often spiritually enriching. We tend to become more sensitive, inclusive of diversity, and naturally curious about worldviews that are different from our own. The richness of friendship and community is enrapturing. Because we're keen to step outside ourselves and inhabit the world of others, our circle of care can also grow in astounding ways—even reaching beyond the human world to include all forms of life.

As with all good things, we can have too much of it. Perspective-taking can run away with itself in this space. We can appreciate different perspectives so much here that we start to suppose nothing is ultimately true. We think, "It's all just a bunch of perspectives, and every perspective is true." In its healthy forms, the capacity to see and appreciate life from diverse points of view engenders great humility. We know what we know, but even what we know is limited by our own inescapable smallness. We realize viscerally that we need the perspectives of others to be truly whole. In the words of the American theologian Paul Knitter, "without Buddha I could not be a Christian."[15] This is a classic fourth-person statement.

In its unhealthy forms, promiscuous perspective-taking leads to chaotic relativism. Everything is as good as everything else. We can't assert value judgments about anything because our values are no more than perspectives in the cosmic heap of other values. Right is wrong from another perspective. Good is evil. "It all depends on your point of view." It's not until we mature in the fourth-person perspective that we learn to prioritize different perspectives into hierarchies again and can call evil "evil" with greater confidence.

Another (ironic) pitfall of the fourth-person perspective is intolerant tolerance. We can see from this style of meaning-making that not only our own perspectives are limited, but society itself is an aggregate of biased perspectives that don't always serve everybody equally. We might notice that climate change is already disproportionately impacting the poor of the world. People of color have historically had a harder time securing a bank loan in the United States. Though animals can't advocate for themselves, there is good evidence that they are capable of suffering and that the meat industry needs an overhaul to reflect this understanding. In short, we're now sensitive to perspectives that were previously marginalized or altogether invisible to us. Out of an abundance of care and compassion, we want to create a world that is more merciful and just. And yet, in our immature zeal, we might condemn anyone who has not yet "woken up" to this way of seeing things. To be a voice for the marginalized of society is a noble vocation. But berating others who don't feel called to be more like us is not a very effective tool for converting hearts. It takes us time to learn this lesson.

I mentioned above that at the mature reaches of the fourth-person perspective, we start to become sensitive to developmental dynamics themselves. That is, we notice the pattern that the person I once took myself to be is now in my view—an object seen by a new subject. At the mature fourth-person perspective, it naturally dawns on us that we are growing in the vertical sense. We come to understand intuitively that vertical development is just part of being a human being—we take one self to the cross as another self emerges from the tomb.

This discovery, for most people, is exhilarating. To be reborn, and to know that we've been reborn, is an inherently spiritual experience. In fact, people at the mature fourth-person perspective tend to have an energy about them, a fire. They feel alive as they knowingly participate in the evolutionary movement of Spirit Itself.

Yet, we often lack the maturity and discernment in this space to know how much to say when and to whom. I've counseled with many students over the years who come to me lamenting how poorly a conversation on "development" went with their parents, their partner, their stake president. Sometimes we get so excited about vertical development that we begin to evangelize it in a way that repels more than it invites.

There are often people in our lives who we desperately want to see us for who we are. If they don't seem as revved up over the stages of faith as we are, we're happy to assign them reading materials to get them up to speed. But how many of us enjoy getting a reading assignment from a loved one that implies we're a defective human being?

Much worse than the temptation to forcibly educate others on human development is the belief that we can't be close with others because *they're not developed enough*. It seems that part of the growing pains of coming to developmental self-awareness is feeling irritated towards those we deem to be less evolved than ourselves. It's a bit like a second adolescence.

To be a vessel of Christic Love is the great calling of the gospel. At the fourth-person perspective, the temptation is to see others as "less developed" than we would like them to be. The irony is that when we take this view, we fail to see our own immaturity in the very act of judgment. But by grace, we learn to see with new eyes. We come to understand that if we don't have access to compassionate awareness in our dealing with others, then the problem is not with them. It's with us. The more we accept ourselves in all our shortcomings, the more readily we fully accept and forgive others in turn. When we remove the beam from our eye, the radiance of the human family and Creation Itself stands shimmering before us.

EXERCISE:

We all notice different aspects of reality. Depending on which aspects we favor and privilege, our worldview will take shape accordingly. Some contexts we are sensitive to while others feel less important. Still, there are other contexts we aren't conscious of at all. Below you can practice bringing more of the contexts that make up who you are into awareness.

PART I: WHAT'S RIGHT ABOUT THIS PERSPECTIVE?

Think of a person who holds a perspective that you find to be challenging or even irritating and patently wrong.

Take some deep breaths, relax through the body, and try to find yourself holding this same view. Ask yourself, What's right about this perspective?

Don't move on until you've connected with the genuine wisdom of this perspective. Feel the way this view, this context is a gift to you, opening you up to an aspect of reality that you were previously closed off to.

PART II: SOCIETAL SYSTEMS

Think about your community, your church, your nation—whichever collective you belong to that has interest for you.

What contexts could you change in this environment in order to allow people to grow to their full potential?

Note: Try to be realistic about this. This isn't a wish list so much as things you can actually imagine changing that would be of benefit to the entire system.

For example, at the community level, what if we had a practice of regularly participating in religious and spiritual traditions other than our own, with no agenda but to connect with another group where we live? What impact would that have on our church "system"? On our community "system"?

FIFTH-PERSON PERSPECTIVE

At the fifth-person perspective, we back off from the language-based, egoic operating system that has been at the center of our meaning-making throughout the human journey. Here, for the first time, we see the activity of the mind churning out perspectives, generating meaning endlessly, only to witness each word, each thought, each concept fall back into the sea of Being like a wave swallowed back into the ocean.

Dr. Susanne Cook-Greuter, who first articulated this stage, called it "construct aware" in a straightforward, descriptive manner: we are aware of the *constructed* nature of all knowledge now—witnessing and experiencing the inner workings of the meaning-making process itself.[16] We begin to see that all we ever experience, all we ever know are the mind's constructs, which are idiosyncratic symbols of a Fullness too vast to ever entirely represent. Perhaps this is why Heraclitus asserted that "God is both willing and unwilling to be called *God*." Willing, because to name things is convenient. Unwilling, because the name can never comprehend the reality it refers to.

Prior to this perspective, we unconsciously assume that what we name with language has inherent and separate existence—Mount Fuji, the US government, Christianity. But we fail to appreciate that language imposes artificial borders and boundaries around all that it names. A concrete example will help us unpack this concept.

Conventionally, I can refer to myself as "Thomas" and get around town just fine. I ask someone else their name, and they usually don't have any trouble responding in turn. "I'm Nancy. Nice to meet you." And we're off to the races. But who we say we are—the story we tell about ourselves—is necessarily a dramatic reduction and oversimplification. My name can't begin to describe the carbon in my cells that was cooked in the crucible of the stars billions of years ago. My name doesn't express the yearning of my ancestors whose dreams, visions, and sacred beliefs still live through me. No name can express the depths of my interiority and the call I feel to live my life in a very particular way. No volume of books could ultimately detail the countless systems—biological, social, cultural, political—that influence, inform, and help give rise to this activity and process I call "Thomas" as a shorthand.

As a matter of convenience, we give things names. When my lunch order is up at the cafe, they want "Thomas" to pick up his salad, not "Nancy." This system creates an economy of understanding where we can communicate with each other and move about in the world, going about our basic tasks.

But at the fifth-person perspective, we start to pull back the curtain, as it were, and appreciate all that lies behind the thin veil of the surface mind's labels. We see in a more stabilized way that *everything is in fact everything*. In Buddhism, the teaching of "dependent arising" expresses that nothing exists without the support of everything else. In Latter-day Saint parlance, Christ's Light is in and through all things. Each thing we call *thing* is in fact an *open-ended process* with *no beginning and no ending*. The wave cannot exist without the ocean. The fifth-person perspective is our first big taste of gliding through the world as an individual wave while also being aware of our inseparability from the ocean.

With this new awareness, I start to ask the following: "Who or what is it that's been aware of moving through these different perspectives along the developmental journey? Who or what was aware of playing in the sandbox when the self's only concern was 'I, me, and mine?' Somehow I backed off of that first-person perspective and started seeing other selves. I was aware of their needs and their wants. I learned how to get along in a family and in a community. Then I took another step back. I became aware of a self forming his own ideas and opinions and deciding what he wanted to do with his one precious life. Later on, I woke up to the contexts and conditions that gave shape to *that* self, the contexts that colored all of his thinking and feeling and dreaming and yearning. What is it that has been aware all along, watching one self die and another be born?"

Until the fifth-person perspective, I have unconsciously identified with the self that is experienced as a sensing body, feeling heart, and thinking mind. But now I am aware of the body-heart-mind as an object in awareness that is constantly evolving, which means I am a new subject looking at the old subject. I'm not just a thinking mind. I'm not just a feeling body. I'm not just the sum total of what I've lived and experienced in the body-heart-mind. I'm not just my hopes, aspirations, and dreams of the future. I'm not just my cultural programming and all of the contexts that influence my seeing. I *am* all those things, but I am also the awareness that's aware of all these objects, all these activities. *What could it possibly mean that I am the awareness that is aware of all experience?* This is the disorienting and inevitable question of the fifth-person perspective. As with every other perspective we've explored, it is a space that comes with both promise and peril.

Gifts of the Fifth-Person Perspective

Several years ago I participated in a group over a nine-month period with a collective intention to explore the very territory I've been describing in this chapter. Among the participants were a number of late-career men who had been very successful in their industries. There was also a woman in her early thirties with dark, cropped hair and a sassy tone who was especially precocious. One day after an intense group process, the woman said in a light and humorous way, "All these men in the group want to build an organization that's going to 'change the world.' *I'm going to change the world by the way I encounter this tree."* This is as iconic an expression from the fifth-person perspective as I've ever heard.

As the solidity of our ideas and concepts hollows out, we come to appreciate the *power of presence*. We feel at the heart of our being that we have the capacity to sanctify each moment with the quality of our awareness. Before, when we were identified with our thoughts, with our constructed sense of self, it was hard to not take that self seriously. It was the only self we knew, after all. But from a fifth-person perspective, we have a new capacity to develop true humility. We ask: Do I really know what I say I know? Isn't this conviction I've been so uptight about my whole life just another construct? While this process of taking inventory of everything we've ever known, believed, or loved can be daunting, it can lead to a place of greater openness and lightness. We take ourselves much less seriously and really learn how to laugh. We learn to cry as well because we can let go of former beliefs that dictated how and when we should cry too.

Perhaps above all, at the fifth-person perspective we have an opportunity to love others with a new quality. We realize that if my true self is the awareness, or Light, that is aware of all experience, is it not the same Light that sees through the eyes of "the other" and feels through their hearts? Are we not of one essence, no matter how different our thoughts, feelings, beliefs, and backgrounds are? When Christ said to love your neighbor as yourself, he couldn't have meant "love your neighbor *as much as* you love yourself." Frankly, we're not all that nice to ourselves half the time. We feel from this new seat of identity that the great commandment is to *love your neighbor as your very own being*. To do this, it helps to be able to see in real time that their essence is one and the same with our own.

Pitfalls of the Fifth-Person Perspective

Of course, drawing from the fifth-person perspective does not guarantee that we will follow the great commandments or even be a decent person for that matter.

One of the confusions of this space is that we struggle to see that while the mind develops constructs to represent different aspects of experience, it does not do so out of thin air. There are deeper patterns to Creation—what we would call "laws" in Latter-day Saint theology—that give rise to the mind's reflections. To learn to move with the flow of this patterning is to learn to become divine. To move against it is to suffer and to deny greater Light. At the mature fifth-person perspective, we learn to intuit these patterns, to cooperate with them and to create through them. But it generally requires a lot of painful stumbling to develop this new ability.

It is not uncommon for individuals to feel significant existential despair in this new space. After all, our whole lives we've thought we were a particular person—the oversimplified, constructed self we took ourselves to be. "I thought I was my thoughts. I thought I was my memories. I thought I was my hopes and dreams. Now all of those mental constructs feel like foamy bubbles washing down a stream."

Heartache is another word I've heard to describe it—a sense of feeling gutted and hollowed out. Many even feel betrayal. "I've lived my whole life thinking I was something that I'm not. I've given all that I have to something that I'm ultimately not."

But those who mourn are also comforted. My personal experience working with Latter-day Saints who test at this range of development is that with the right kind of support, they come to express a radiant sense of ease about them. Some are humorous and spontaneous, while others are philosophical and penetrating in their wisdom. Most of them I've found have a great ability to connect with others and see the inherent dignity in each person's life.

Lived with faith and a brightness of hope, this perspective can reveal an even greater majesty in Divine Life than we had previously imagined.[17]

FROM FIFTH- TO SIXTH-PERSON PERSPECTIVE[18]

As the fifth-person perspective matures, we see a flowering of complexity. Even though we're aware that all human knowledge is constructed—that is, mediated and represented by the mind—we learn to have *confidence in constructs*. We start to work across entire systems as fluidly as a child manipulates and combines different colors of play dough. One individual at the late fifth-person perspective may bend all of the power of his spirit on raising a child in novel ways, combining modalities as diverse as art therapy, polyvagal theory, and nature-based education. Another person may reimagine the global economic system by starting with an assumption of resource abundance rather than resource scarcity.

The late fifth-person perspective represents maximal complexity in the life of mind. This complexity is perhaps the case because at this stage, we're capable of moving smoothly across systems and worldviews without being captured by the reality or finality of any particular perspective. Just as a lucid dreamer is not bound by a single dreamscape, the waking dreamer at this stage conjures up one world after another.

On the other side of this complexity, we enter the great simplicity of the sixth-person perspective. We see that for all the mind's complexity and endless possibilities that flow from it, they are all just constructs in the end. And all constructs are a single substance. Call it "Light," call it "Consciousness," call it nothing at all. Lex Hixon writes, "All forms that manifest within the One are only, in the words of Plotinus, *the clear light which is Itself.* There is only the One."[19]

While humans can have unitive, or nondual, experience from quite an early time in life (as early as the second-person perspective perhaps), it's at the sixth-person perspective where unitive perception becomes a stage feature. That is, it becomes an enduring trait, not a passing state. In practice, this means a human being who is mature at the sixth-person perspective will experience all of Creation as one seamless (but not featureless!) Bloom. The self remains real but is only one particular eddy in the Stream of all that is.   All the way up through the fifth-person perspective, there remains a sense that it's "my awareness." It feels as though I am processing the experience that's happening to *me*. At the sixth-person perspective, *Experiencing experiences Experiencing*; Light alone knows Light. Yes, there is still a unique self, but it is a drop-of-water self comprised of the same wetness as the entire Ocean. Before, I was aware of the Ocean. Now I *am* the Ocean. *We* are Ocean.

In Doctrine and Covenants, this Unitive Reality is named as the Light of Christ, which "is in the sun, and the light of the sun, and the power thereof by which it was made. As also . . . in the moon, and is the light of the moon, and the power thereof by which it was made; As also the light of the stars, and the power thereof by which they were made; And the earth also, and the power thereof, even the earth upon which you stand. And the light which shineth, which giveth you light, is through him who enlighteneth your eyes, which is the same light that quickeneth your understandings" (Doctrine and Covenants 88:7–11). This scripture is not just religious poetry. It is not speculative theology. We see this and feel this as naturally as we breathe from the sixth-person perspective.

As with all stages, there are virtues and pitfalls to this new potential. With the separate self now rendered translucent by the Light of its own substance, we can open up to a nonstriving acceptance in this space that wasn't possible to this degree before. Separation of any kind is seen to be illusory. The felt experience of Being is one of participating in an Infinite and Eternal Love. Spontaneous knowing that bears the aesthetic patterning of the Universe itself can erupt into consciousness without warning, manifesting as a rare form of creativity at this stage. People I've spoken with who abide in this space describe the experience as a kind of cosmic "download," where they receive a vision fully formed that may take them years to articulate and represent using conventional human means. By way of challenges, imagine a wobbly Jenga tower that represents zero- through sixth-person perspectives now. If I have unresolved issues at the third-person perspective and have never felt truly accomplished, that "hole" in my Jenga tower will tend to create instability all the way up. To the extent I suffered an attachment injury at the first-person perspective, I may feel cosmically at ease in one moment only to experience intense abandonment and volatility in the next. The energy centers don't go away. Our vulnerabilities remain vulnerable as long as we're embodied human beings. The difference is at the sixth-person perspective, I may be so liberated from the body-heart-mind's pains and pleasures that I rarely become reactive, even when intense signals are activating through the open Field of consciousness.

But this very liberation can also be a liability. Perhaps God is communicating to us through our third-person "radio bandwidth" that there is a task to be accomplished. But I, having a preference now for cosmic bliss, can tune that message out and escape back into a Oneness where nothing needs to be done. Everything is just fine as it is. To the extent that I am not fully embodied through all the stages and perspectives, I run the risk of spiritual bypass. When things get hard and life calls me to action, I may choose to bliss out instead.

But with a supportive community and by Grace, we can bloom into something that seems rather fantastic to most people at this point in our human history. We can come to know our own invincible Wholeness. A quality of immediacy and intimacy with all Creation naturally arises at this stage—all of Joy and Sorrow, all of Agony and Ecstasy. The largest galaxy is no different in essence than the smallest grain of sand. Everything is revealed. All things testify of Him by whose Power all is created. Creation takes the form of Life, Love, and Light as an expression of Its own boundless creativity. The sheer multiplicity and diversity of the Divine movement is testament to its

Eternal Oneness. The One and the Many are not two in the end. We take a shower, we walk our dog, we cook a meal for a friend, and nowhere in the experience of showering or walking the dog or cooking is any part of the entire cosmos excluded from our company. The ordinary is truly extraordinary.

THE HARVEST

Studying the territory of human development has been an ongoing source of revelation for me and has deepened my relationship with the Divine more than I can express. Still, more than ever, I try to be aware of the pitfalls (and hubris) of attempting to chart human growth and progress.

I've come to feel that it's wise not to underemphasize the importance of vertical development—linear, hierarchical growth from the zero- through sixth-person perspective—but not to overemphasize it either. When we underemphasize development, one narrow way of viewing the gospel can become dominant while other legitimate and faithful perspectives become marginalized. On the other hand, if we overemphasize development, we tend to idealize the later stages, devalue the earlier ones, and even feel inadequate that we're not at a different stage than we are. Both approaches miss the mark.

This map I've shared (which is just a construct) can help clarify and illuminate certain patterns and potentials in our human-divine development. However, it is not designed to tell us anything about how pleasing our lives are before God. That involves a different dimension of maturity entirely, which I've called "virtue" in other parts of this book.

And yet vertical development and virtue are not wholly divorced constructs. They do have a relationship. As we grow up, new virtues and divine qualities become available for us to cultivate. As we "grow down," we hone and refine those qualities that are already an embodied aspect of our being. In both growing up and growing down, we increase in being. We receive more Light and grow brighter and brighter until the perfect day. Expressed another way, wherever we are, whatever our degree of conversion, the Divine seems to have ample means to make us holy, if we're willing.

At this time we are living in, there is new knowledge as well as ongoing revelation regarding what it means to transform—to become a *new creature* animated by Christ. If we are open-minded and open-hearted, we will see with new eyes what virtues and gifts are already ripening through our individual and collective life. I see the great invitation before us as this: to further build a Zion community that honors and supports the cultivation of divine gifts across the entire spectrum of consciousness—Life, Love and Light; zero- through sixth-person perspectives; and beyond.

The fields are ripe. The spiritual radiance of our community will be the harvest.

MEDITATION
Infinite Life in Christ

Chapter 7

At-One-Ment

THROUGHOUT THIS BOOK, I've intended to convey a simple message that I take to be at the heart of the gospel: We are not who we thought we were. Who we are is so infinite, it is beyond thought and belief altogether. In his ministry, Jesus called us to our Infinite Nature by announcing the arrival of the kingdom of heaven. When we turn toward it (*metanoia*), we become one with the Divine, one with our own *Christ Nature* (at-one-ment).

By "Christ Nature," I mean to emphasize that Jesus the human, at a cosmically ripe and opportune moment, joined himself fully with us, with God, and with all of Creation. His at-one-ment was not a one-off act so much as a capacity that he grew into, in time. Through Joseph Smith, the Apostle John bore witness of Jesus's gradual growth: "And he received not of the fulness at first, but continued from grace to grace, until he received a fulness; And thus he was called the Son of

God, because he received not of the fulness at the first" (Doctrine and Covenants 93:13–14).

Jesus not only *was* the Christ since before time and space were born (see Colossians 1:15), but he *became* the Christ in earthly life through His faithfulness. Evolving into a fully realized being, he showed us through his life and death what we too are capable of becoming by way of Grace. Not only did he show us our own Christ Nature by more fully realizing his, he taught us, as all master teachers do, that we can do even better: "I tell you the truth, anyone who believes in me will do the same works I have done, and even greater works" (John 14:12, NLT).

To realize our true nature, Christ asks us to take up our cross and join Him in death. It will be the death of a self-that-we-are-not. And when we die, we rise as a new self, as sons and daughters of Eternity, being ever more as Christ is—One with the Father, the Mother, and All that is.

This process will not occur *later*. It is *at hand* already, immanent in the fullness of our embodiments.

Paul wrote with great force: "Have you forgotten that when we were joined with Christ Jesus in baptism, we joined him in his death? For we died and were buried with Christ by baptism. And just as Christ was raised from the dead by the glorious power of the Father, now we also may live new lives" (Romans 6:3–4, NLT). Though we are afraid to die to the self and world we know, new Life beckons us. The soul is somehow under the sway of this strange *Gravity*. Christ's Infinite Body pulls on the hearts of every being just as the moon pulls on the ocean. We feel in the churning of our marrow there is a greater Love we're called to become.

To at-one, then, is not a singular act so much as a *natural process*. It is the nature of Nature. Atonement stands revealed in the evolving reality of Christ and in our own developing godhood, that all may be One.

A LOOK BACK AT SOME KEY LANDMARKS

We've covered a lot of ground in the previous chapters. The divine-human living in Sacredness is a reality too full for words. Any map will inevitably be an oversimplification of the territory. But as I've argued, a good map can help. By way of review, I want to distill a few of the key points from each chapter—offering you a legend to the map, if you will.

- Alongside ordinary waking reality, there is an entirely new dimension to human life that is available to us. Sometimes by pure Grace we fall into it. But often, it takes some deliberate effort and practice to learn to live in this new realm in an enduring way.

- One reason we fail to appreciate this alternate dimension—the kingdom within us—is that we've been trained to live life boxed up in the thinking mind. When we confuse our *true identity* with thought, we get anxious and feel separate from others, even separate and alienated from our Sacred Source.

- In order to wake up from this sleep and confusion, we can start to pay more attention to the different ways of knowing, the different qualities of Intelligence that comprise our human-divinity. These include (but are not limited to) the knowing of the body, heart, mind, and conscious Spirit, or awareness itself.

- For complex evolutionary reasons, the mind operates with many distinct intentions and agendas at any given time. This ability is good for survival but hard on our spiritual life and well-being. To open our "eye of wisdom," we need to train ourselves out of the fragmented state of a chronically distracted mind.

- Concentration, therefore, is a foundational skill in spiritual life. When we've learned to steady our attention, we can keep an *eye single* on what matters most for as long as we choose. With a unified mind, we can get used to greater degrees of Glory.

- The heart's knowing is critically important on the path of discipleship. To paraphrase the Apostle Paul, the realities of the sacred heart can only be communicated by the words of the heart (cf. 1 Corinthians 2:13). The thinking mind will often fail to perceive the realities that an open, awake heart reveals to us in plain daylight.

- Just as we learn to work with the forces of distraction when training the mind, we purify the heart by filtering out the "noise" of egocentric emotions and attuning to the baseline "signal" of Divine Love. In this way the heart becomes increasingly receptive and open to transformative spiritual currents.

- As human beings, our higher ideals are entangled with our wounded, animal bodies. To take up residence in the kingdom of heaven, we have to be honest and humble about our wounding, about when we feel disturbed and tempted to act out. The core vulnerabilities of our humanity point to the precise places in ourselves where we're primed to receive the most Grace and Light. God calls us to greater holiness *through* our tribulations, making weak things become strong (see Ether 12:27).

- The world is not what it seems. We are not who we thought we were. Modern developmental psychology reveals a new, multiperspectival view of the gospel. From each distinct perspective and stage of development, new challenges and possibilities in the life of the self become apparent. Each perspective brings with it enormous spiritual potentials and gifts as well as potential pitfalls and blind spots.

- Understanding the spectrum of divine-human development—Life, Love, and Light—can help us more fully engage in a life of ongoing progression, right here and now.

EXPECT DRAMATIC RESULTS

Shinzen Young, a longtime Buddhist teacher of mine, is fond of telling his students that they should "expect dramatic results" from spiritual practice. I love this language and the way it shakes us all out of our complacency. The opposite of expecting dramatic results is something like following the same regimen every day in a safe and controlled environment. It amounts to insulating ourselves from a Glory that would set our hearts ablaze if we would let it.

I've found too often that we do this as Latter-day Saints, domesticating our spiritual lives and assuming the most dramatic spiritual transformations will occur after we die. But what if some of the most dramatic changes occur right here in this very human life? What if we've been squandering this precious opportunity for full embodiment out of a misguided sense that this life is about clinging to a fixed set of beliefs and *enduring to the end*? Isn't *enduring* this life setting the bar a bit low?

The words of Amulek would seem to support the attitude of radical transformation: "Now is the time and the day of your salvation; and therefore, if ye will repent and harden not your hearts, *immediately* shall the great plan of redemption be brought about unto you" (Alma 34:31; emphasis added). The logic of the mind tells us that *eventually* we can be saved. The mind cannot help but understand truth in terms of linear sequences, one thing occurring after another. But the heart's knowing is *immediate* and *instantaneous*. No sooner do we repent—that is, *go beyond our former sense of self*—than we open our eyes to a new dimension of reality. It is the very realm that Christ has been calling us to. The good stuff doesn't come later. The dramatic results are always *now*. Salvation and redemption are effective *immediately*. The question as always on this inner path is, do we have eyes to see? What world do we take ourselves to be living in?

Another way of saying "expect dramatic results" is "this path is highly reliable when you follow it." You can trust it with your whole being. What path is that? Amulek described it succinctly as "faith unto repentance." Christ's whole intent in His "last sacrifice" was to bring about "means unto men that they may have *faith unto repentance*" (Alma 34:15; emphasis added). What meaning can we make of this phrase "faith unto repentance"?

So often we equate faith with belief. But I like to understand faith as *free fall*. In a quote widely attributed to Chögyam Trungpa Rinpoche, one of the great Tibetan Buddhist masters of the twentieth century, he states humorously: "The bad news is you're falling through the air, nothing to hang on to, no parachute. The good news is, there's no ground." In Latter-day Saint theology, I would amend his statement only slightly: We are falling indeed. Christ is the Gravity causing us to fall upward into our infinite potential. There is no ground because there is no end to Christ and to what we are capable of becoming. But we still have to be willing to let go of control and to fall.

When we exercise faith as free fall, we take "no thought for the morrow" (Matthew 6:34, KJV). Whether we live or die, we belong to the Lord (see Romans 14:8, NLT). When we let ourselves go into this free fall, repentance—*metanoia*—follows naturally. Remember that *metanoia* points to going beyond the small self that is dogged by an insatiable need for safety, pleasure, esteem, and control. In the logic of the small self, we maintain a sense of safety and control by always having all the right answers, being a member of the winning tribe, and earning salvation based on good performance.

Beyond this small self is a *big Self*, one that is poor in spirit and pure in heart. As the big Self, we voluntarily give up control as an act of faith. We enter a free fall in this new atmosphere and find ourselves falling up, not down. In Christ's gravitational field, we come to understand that Love is our very substance as well as our ultimate destination.

When we sincerely practice faith unto repentance, sooner or later we experience a loss of certainty about who we actually are. I'm aware that this teaching flies in the face of some of the cultural instruction we've received. From a young age we're taught to know exactly who we are, as well as where we're from, why we're here, and where we're going. There is a time and a season for that orientation. But there is also a time in life to know and a time in life to not know.

We need a healthy amount of containment and control in life, especially in our formative years when we're coming into our sense of self. It's good to know the answers to life's most basic questions. The more black and white, in fact, the better. But after we've developed a healthy sense of self, then the practice of submission becomes all-important. Later in life, we have the opportunity to sacrifice who we thought we were for something even better. All of this is to say that pure faith is profoundly risky. We risk losing everything we thought we knew for something even better. We exercise faith that Christ's Reality is better than anything we can possibly imagine.

If we trick ourselves into believing we're more certain than we actually are, we unwittingly energize our need to feel safe and trade an infinitely greater good for a false sense of security. We think we're showing faith when in fact we're exercising doubt by refusing to let go of control—to enter free fall. Such is the stealthiness of the energy centers.

The opposite of dramatic results in spiritual life are *predictable results*. We do the same thing over and over. And though we're no longer energized by our well-worn beliefs and routines, deep down our natural man is comforted to be in control, to not have to take any real risks.

What would it be like, then, if we threw caution to the wind, and let go of our need to know, our need to be in control? The results would be nothing less than dramatic.

PRACTICE:

Sit with the following questions with an open heart and an open mind:

Have I been pretending to know more than I actually know? Have I been trying to control any outcomes that are not mine to control?

See what comes to you. Notice your feelings and impressions. Write.

YESTERDAY'S TONIC IS TODAY'S TOXIN

To the extent that we are a mystery to ourselves, to the extent that we are willing to enter a free fall into Christ's Gravity, the terms of our spiritual life will change continually. Part of us—the part of us that loves to control—will want everything to stay put and to always know the answers to life's most important questions. But Sacred Reality has bigger plans for us than that. Like Paul, we are asked to "die daily" (1 Corinthians 15:31, KJV).

Developmentally, if we allow ourselves to move freely from one transformation to the next according to divine timing, the path can't help but assume new forms across different inflection points in life. What we need for our spiritual growth will change over time if we let it. But we can trust the Sacred to provide. The great Hindu sage Sri Aurobindo wrote with unsurpassable faith:

> There are things which were beneficial, helpful, which seemed perhaps at one time the one thing desirable, and yet once their work is done, once they are attained, they become obstacles and even hostile forces when we are called to advance beyond them. There are desirable states of the soul which it is dangerous to rest in after they have been mastered, because then we do not march on to the wider kingdoms of God beyond. . . . We must rest at nothing less than the All, nothing short of the utter transcendence. And if we can thus be free in the spirit, we shall find out all the wonder of God's workings; we shall find that in inwardly renouncing everything we have lost nothing.[1]

This is a stunning call to trust in Sacred Reality absolutely. If we renounce *everything*, we will have lost *nothing*. We are as the lilies of the field: "If God cares so wonderfully for wildflowers that are here today and thrown into the fire tomorrow, he will certainly care for you. Why do you have so little faith?" (Matthew 6:30, NLT). Why do we hedge our bets in spiritual life? Why do we fear losing control of who we think we are? Why do we wish to build bigger barns for our harvest as an insurance plan against tomorrow's unknown (cf. Luke 12:16–21)?

In chapter five we spent considerable time on the energy centers, contemplating our core vulnerabilities. When we operate from the logic of our human weakness, we will always want more security, pleasure, esteem, and power. These appetites can come to dominate our lives if we fail to go beyond the reality of the small self (*metanoia*).

We often want to rest in the things that worked spiritually yesterday because we feel safe when we think we have the right formula dialed in. I call this "getting stuck in a good place." We're doing fine, but we're afraid of what might happen if we risk the modest comforts we've secured for the Unknown. So we reinforce our position.

But the notion that "what worked yesterday should work today" is static. And our static thoughts and beliefs can never keep pace with an always-evolving Divine Reality. Remaining stuck in our patterning and habits is spiritual death. Christ asks us to take this habituated self to the cross. He wants us to understand for ourselves that no law, no matter how scrupulously observed, can save us. We are meant to become more than our impulses, fears, and routines.

As Christ lives through us in increasing measure, we become more dynamic, more creative, more *alive*. He speaks to all of us when he says, "I am come that they might have life, and that they might have it more abundantly" (John 10:10, KJV). The more alive we become, the more unknowable to ourselves we are. The less predictable we are. We surprise ourselves by doing things and saying things that we didn't know we were capable of. Jesus describes this freedom and spontaneity when he says, "The wind blows wherever it pleases. You hear its sound, but you cannot tell where it comes from or where it is going. So it is with everyone born of the Spirit" (John 3:8, NIV).

From a creaturely perspective, we want homeostasis and predictability. We want things not too hot and not too cold. We want what worked yesterday to work today as well. We resist change. But from the view of infinite Life in Christ, it is inevitable that what worked for us yesterday in spiritual life will give way to *truer* truths today. It can be frightening to accommodate this wide-open way of life in the gospel. Here, there are no walls, no ceilings, and no floors. The sensation of free fall can feel overwhelmingly insecure from the ego's limited perspective. But we can trust that a more expansive Beauty awaits on the other side of our insatiable need for security. When we advance beyond the *hostile forces* of yesterday's comforts, we will "march on to the wider kingdoms of God beyond."

REFLECTIVE JOURNALING:

Can you sense any personal or spiritual practices that once felt very rewarding to you but now feel outworn? What about new spiritual habits, practices, or intuitions that haven't fully taken root that, nevertheless, you feel called to nurture?

JUST MESSING AROUND WITH THE EGO

All this dying and being reborn can sometimes feel like a lot to manage. Where do we even begin? There is a summary teaching I want to offer here. If you forget everything else, you can work with this one thing, and it will take you far.

One day, a longtime teacher of mine, John Kesler, said spontaneously in the flow of conversation: "If you ever experience anything but compassion towards someone, you're just messing around with the ego." The weight of what he said impacted me like a meteor crashing into the ocean, sending heaving tidal waves in every direction.

The implication is that our fundamental nature *is* compassion. God is Love, and we are Love's means. But clearly we don't show up as Divine Love in every situation. We're often less than loving towards ourselves and others. How do we account for this? If our nature is Divine Compassion, what is it that obscures and distorts this nature?

I mentioned previously the psychological process of projection. When we project, we attribute qualities to others that are in fact our own qualities. But for different reasons, we're not yet ready to take responsibility for ourselves. We can't yet admit to ourselves, let alone to others, that these qualities are a part of who we are.

For me, personally, it wasn't until I was well into my thirties that I was even remotely willing to admit what a selfish person I could be. Other people's selfishness was readily apparent to me, of course.

When I was feeling generous, I was even willing to give "those people" advice on how they could stop being so selfish. With the help of some challenging relationships, high-quality mentoring, and Love's Gravity in general, it slowly dawned on me that I become reactive when I see selfishness in others precisely because I wasn't willing to see it in myself. Another way of saying this is that I was already experiencing selfishness all the time in my day-to-day life. But because I was so invested in not having a *conscious* relationship with my own selfishness, the only option left for me was to *unconsciously* relate to selfishness through other people.

Projection is not all bad news, though. We don't just project our negative qualities onto others because we're prideful people who refuse to remove the log from our own eye. Projection often serves as a healthy defense mechanism that allows us to form a healthy, positive sense of self, especially in our formative years.[2] None of us can stare down our demons all at once.

But eventually, after we've stabilized in a healthy sense of self, it becomes possible to uncover some of the material we necessarily had to repress through the developmental process in order to form positive self-esteem. For me personally, this means that nowadays, I'm generally less reactive when I experience others being selfish. Because I have a more conscious relationship with my own selfishness, and am even compassionate towards that weakness of mine to an extent, when I see it in others, I can offer the same quality of compassion. Rather than the knee-jerk attitude of hostility towards selfishness, I might have the thought, "They must be in a tough spot if they can't see how their actions are hurting others right now. I know I hurt others all the time without knowing it. I wonder if there's something I can do to be helpful."

Projection doesn't only stem from our negative, unflattering qualities. We project our virtue and spiritual talents on to others as well. Have you ever known someone in your life for whom you feel intense admiration? In fact, you see them as being so good they start to take on a saintly, almost otherworldly air? This form of disturbance is a telltale sign that we're refusing to take ownership of our own goodness.

Just as I wasn't seeing my own selfishness but could readily see it in others, oftentimes we can't see our own lovingness, patience, or capacity to forgive. As a result, we feel a disproportionate admiration for another person precisely because we've lost contact with this very quality in ourselves. Again, we don't do this because we're bad people. In fact, we might just not be ready to take full responsibility for the divine beings we are, capable of blessing others without end.

In the case of this "golden shadow" practice—coming into conscious relationship with our virtue—we can notice that the qualities we most love and admire in our spiritual heroes are also our own qualities. Once we've done this work, we'll likely continue to feel admiration and love towards this person, but it will be an appropriate and empowering love, not one that puts another on a pedestal and leaves us groveling below.

There is one more powerful movement in this sequence that one of my favorite stories in the New Testament illustrates beautifully. A rich man runs up to Jesus, kneels down, and says, "Good teacher, what must I do to inherit eternal life?" Though the rest of the account is moving and edifying, it's Jesus's initial response that I find to be so powerful. "'Why do you call me good?' Jesus asked. 'Only God is truly good'" (Mark 10:17–18, NLT).

As we're forming a sense of self, there is a time when it is skillful to *disown* our negative qualities. Once we've developed into a stable enough ego identity with healthy self-esteem, we can re-own these qualities and, as a result, can be more compassionate to ourselves and others. At the level of Self beyond self (true repentance, *metanoia*), there is nothing to disown or to own. We let go of even the notion that "we" are good and recognize that Sacred Reality is the Goodness by which we are good.

What were those negative qualities to begin with then? They are something like the fears of a self who hasn't yet learned to turn towards the intensity of God's Presence. When we awaken from that bad dream, we see Goodness everywhere, and we see others who we can help awaken from their private nightmares in turn.

I can sum up this practice in a few simple words: When you see something disturbing that you want to judge, recognize, "That's me." When you see something beautiful and virtuous, "That's me too." Beyond "that's me," we see clearly that Sacred Reality alone is Good.

LIFE PRACTICE:
PART I: SHADOW WORK

Notice the moments when you're less than compassionate towards others. What quality do you perceive in them that disturbs you? Notice the judgment you have about the person or about that specific quality. If it helps, you can work with the following sentence stem: "The quality that most disturbs me in this person is his/her/their _____." Just write it all out, and be honest about your genuine experience. Feel the disturbance in your body. Feel the sensations associated with it. Really feel it, and let the energy move.

Next, let go of your focus on the other person. Bring awareness to yourself, and stay present until you can locate the very same quality in yourself. Breathe into it, acknowledge that you also have this same disturbing quality, and hold an intention to relate to it with more compassion.

Finally, bring your attention back to the person that you found disturbing a moment ago. How do they appear to you after you've removed the beam from your own eye?

Note that wherever you go from here, whether you pursue a relationship with the person or not, you can now act from a place of more compassion.

Also note that it's not uncommon to need to work through this exercise many times before you've really internalized the insights from it.

PART II: GOLDEN SHADOW

You can carry out this same process towards people you feel intense admiration for. Notice the very positive disturbance you feel, and reflect on the quality that inspires you so much. "What I most admire about this person is his/her/their _____." Once again, really feel the sensations that come up in the body here. Let them fully express themselves.

When you're ready, bring awareness to your interiors, and find the same quality in yourself that you love so much in the other. Maybe it's a lesser magnitude of the same quality, maybe it's less mature. Nevertheless, clearly see and feel that you possess the same seed of divine quality within you.

ABBREVIATED VERSION: "THAT'S ME"

Notice when you feel reactive to other people and any of their qualities that you have judgments about. Not just negative judgments but positive judgments too. Practice saying, "That's me." Then, in a very earnest way, find that very quality in yourself. Someone's anger, someone's pettiness, someone's powerful presence, compassion, and selfless service: "That's me."

LIVING STONES

Peter describes Christ in the New Testament as the "living cornerstone of God's temple" (1 Peter 2:4, NLT). And the rest of us, he goes on to say, "are living stones that God is building into his spiritual temple" (1 Peter 2:5, NLT).

There are two elements in this scripture I'd like to reflect on. The first is the concept of *livingness*. Under ordinary circumstances, a stone is the opposite of something we would take to be "living." But in

Peter's metaphor, stones are brought to life in Christ. Through Him, they become something completely different in essence. By extension, when Christ truly lives in each of us, our fundamental nature is transformed. We take up life and residence in a new realm of being. This is the kingdom. For a stone to wake up and come to life would be a dramatic transformation indeed. But for a human being to shake off the sleep of sin and mortality and live a life in Christ is no less dramatic a metamorphosis.

Not only are we living stones—human beings whose nature is fundamentally transformed in Christ—but we are stones *that God is building into His spiritual temple.* This is the second element of the scripture I'd like to reflect on. Not only are we animated by Divine Life, Love, and Light, but simultaneously we are gathered up in our divine substance for a collective purpose—namely, for the purpose of forming a spiritual house and offering to God. Each one of us is but one stone in a living and holy house. Christ as cornerstone is meaningless without us, the living stones, to complete the structure. Likewise, a single stone, no matter how alive, is not and can never be a complete temple in and of itself.

The impact of Peter's image is twofold: In Christ we are brought to life. And, this divine life cannot be understood apart from collective participation. It's to say that everything we've explored throughout this book—from training our mind to be single to God's glory, to purifying the heart, to confronting our original wounding more honestly—means nothing if we do not consecrate our lives, our *livingness*, in what Paul called the body of Christ. We are not holy until we are *holy together* and unite our unique personhood in a sacred and divine purpose.

MEDITATION
Life, Love, and Light

UNIQUELY PERSONAL, UNIVERSALLY DIVINE

Paul expounds on the new spiritual reality that Christ has made possible: "There are different kinds of spiritual gifts, but the same Spirit is the source of them all. There are different kinds of service, but we serve the same Lord. God works in different ways, but it is the same God who does the work in all of us. A spiritual gift is given to each of us so we can help each other" (1 Corinthians 12:4–7, NLT).

Though there are many gifts in our spiritual community, they are in fact only one gift, a gift of the one Spirit, the Sacred Source. In his masterpiece, *Coming Home*, Lex Hixon comments on the significance of Paul's teaching: "This mystical *life in Christ* is not for solitary sages but is to be reflected fully in the daily life of an extended spiritual family—men, women, and children who share the consciousness of their unity with the Divine. . . . Within this extended family there is a rich diversity of viewpoints and gifts, harmonized in the wholeness of the Divine Nature shared fully by all."[3] Most significantly, Hixon goes on to write: "Paul is not speaking metaphorically but from direct spiritual perception of human beings as the Divine Body."[4]

Herein lies the key. It might be tempting to read Paul's teaching as mere metaphor. We say we're a collective body, but in fact believe that we are many bodies with discrete spiritual gifts and even discrete spiritual fates. We're rather inured to the idea that some of us will be saved and some of us will not. Hixon's reading of Paul, which I wholeheartedly embrace, is more radical. We are in fact one Divine Body. If we cannot see this, to borrow from William Blake, it is because the *doors of our perception* have not yet been cleansed.[5] It is because we have not yet awakened to this divine life which Christ has ushered in. It is because we remain asleep in a false sense of self that was never who we really were to begin with. When we wake up to our Christ Nature and practice *at-one-ment*, a theme we have been exploring throughout this book, "then our sense of separate individuality is attenuated without destroying our special function in the whole."[6] In Paul's words, "yes there are many parts, but only one body. The eye can never say to the hand, 'I don't need you.' The head can't say to the feet, 'I don't need you'" (1 Corinthians 12:20-21, NLT).

There is a paradox at the heart of this path, at the heart of Christ's gospel. We are all uniquely personal, one-of-a-kind images of Divine Parents who feel infinite pride in our very Beingness. Born of Christ's Light, we are all given gifts utterly unique to us that we are called to cultivate and bring forth.

At the very same time, we are not individuals at all. We directly participate in the Universally Divine Presence. To say that we *participate* in Divine Presence is still a concession of language and doesn't get at the radicality of our Oneness with the Sacred. We are emanations of the Divine, not humans seeking spirit so much as *Spirit having a human experience of seeking*. "We" are no more separable from the Divine than a wave from the ocean, than the sun's heat and light from the sun itself. If Christ is God's Son, then we are God's Sonship and Daughtership, all of us, collectively, forever. The nobility of a single soul ennobles us all. The perdition of another amounts to a diminishment of our communal Light.

Joseph Smith wrote that "by proving contraries, truth is made manifest."[7] The Uniquely Personal and Universally Divine are two such contraries. Neither can be fully true or powerful without Its counterpart.

Perhaps the sensibility we find dissonant in some Eastern traditions is the insistence on being one with Reality but then leaving no room for the personal. If we are just universally one with the Ultimate, then we never come to know the personal. Adam and Eve's Fall from the garden is reduced to *maya*—an illusion. There is no path whereby our God seed can mature into our full stature of *unique* divinity. On the other hand, if we only know the uniquely personal then we are severed from our participation in the Divine Nature and we become estranged from our true identity. Sacred Reality is a stranger to us. Our neighbors and fellow human beings appear to us as irreconcilably *other*, with no means of bridging the existential gulf. The portals of heaven close and through a veil of forgetfulness we lose the delicious taste of Oneness.

Embracing both sides of this polarity—the Uniquely Personal and Universally Divine—we can become what we are meant to become precisely because we remember what we've always been in our essence—*the Light in and through all things*. In *One-ing* of opposites, we feel spontaneous reverence for the infinite forms of Divine Incarnation even as we embrace all of Creation with a Love that is no respecter of persons.

This is Zion by any other name: a community of beings waking up to our unique personhood while knowing this personhood to be inescapably constituted by Divine Life, Love, and Light. We read in the Pearl of Great Price, "And the Lord called his people Zion, because they were of one heart and one mind, and dwelt in righteousness; and there was no poor among them" (Moses 7:18). So often we read the phrase "one heart and one mind" and give it a weak interpretation, taking it to point to a consensus where everybody agrees with everyone else all the time and never fails to speak in soft tones. Or worse, we give it a mushy, metaphorical meaning, which lets us off the hook altogether. But in the vein of Lex Hixon, I argue that it cannot merely be metaphor. This verse is pointing directly to our awakened nature in Sacred Reality—the Sacred Heart-Mind that is the Divine Womb of all Creation, of all gods and goddesses. *And we are That.* When we awaken to this Reality, the Sacred speaks through and animates our uniqueness. The Sacred weaves our gifts together in an enlightened community of Divine Exchange. There are no poor among us because Sacred Reality, by definition, is Supreme Abundance, *and we are That.*

As the light of Christ manifests more fully through us, we realize that we cannot stand the slightest separation, the slightest suffering in the world. Absolutely nobody is to be left out of this community of divine giving and receiving. We cannot be complete until every last soul, spirit, and particle of Light is gathered back up in full awareness in Christ.

Gregory of Nyssa, a bishop in the fourth century who is venerated as a saint in many traditions, expressed this potent Reality in the following way: "When perfect love has driven out fear, or fear has been transformed into love, then everything that has been saved will be a unity growing together through the one and only Fullness, and everyone will be, in one another, a unity in the . . . Holy Spirit. . . . In this way, encircled by the unity of the Holy Spirit as the bond of peace, all will be one body and one spirit (Patrologia Graeca 44, 1116).[8]

This "one and only Fullness" is the perfection that we already are, right now, if we could only believe the good news. The kingdom of heaven is *already so close*, if we would only turn towards it.

Atonement is a continual One-ing—in ever-widening rings—with all of ourselves, all beings, and all of Sacred Reality. Though this *simplicity* will cost us everything, the more we give ourselves to it, the more we will realize it is all our hearts have ever yearned for.

What we create together as "one body and one spirit" on the other side of Eternity, I trust, is a greater intensity than we are yet able to bear.

Endnotes

CHAPTER 1

1. Joseph Smith History, vol. E-1, 1666, The Joseph Smith Papers, accessed May 15, 2023, https://www.josephsmithpapers.org/paper-summary/history-1838-1856-volume-e-1-1-july-1843-30-april-1844/36.

2. Shunryu Suzuki, *Zen Is Right Here: Teaching Stories and Anecdotes of Shunryu Suzuki*, ed. David Chadwick (Boulder, CO: Shambhala Publications, 2021), 1.

CHAPTER 2

1. Joseph Henrich, Steven J. Heine, and Ara Norenzayan, "The Weirdest People in the World?," *Behavioral and Brain Sciences* 33, no. 2–3 (June 2010): 61–83, https://doi.org/10.1017/S0140525X0999152X.

2. A term I borrow from the Enneagram tradition and work of G. I. Gurdjieff. For a beautiful primer on the centers of intelligence, see Cynthia Bourgeault, *The Wisdom Way of Knowing: Reclaiming an Ancient Tradition to Awaken the Heart* (Jossey-Bass, 2003).

3. Pierre Teilhard de Chardin, *Hymn of the Universe* (New York: Harpercollins College Div., 1969).

4. Dallin H. Oaks, "The Challenge to Become," *Ensign*, November 2000, https://www.churchofjesuschrist.org/study/general-conference/2000/10/the-challenge-to-become?lang=eng.

5. Maurice Nicoll, *Psychological Commentaries on the Teachings of Gurdjieff and Ouspensky*, vol. 5 (Boulder, CO: Shambhala, 1984), 543.

6. Throughout the rest of the book, I will make liberal use of the New Living Translation (NLT) of the Bible. As a teacher, I've found that the plain, vernacular English of the NLT helps students and readers get right to the essential meaning without stumbling over any archaisms. Where I feel other translations are illuminating, I will make use of those as well.

7. "Apostles' Creed," Christian Reformed Church, accessed June 20, 2023, https://www.crcna.org/welcome/beliefs/creeds/apostles-creed.

8. Though English pronouns funnel us into "he," "she," and "they," I take "Christ" to be an all-embracing Force that integrates the full spectrum of masculine and feminine.

9. I use the Greek spelling to make a distinction between the physical organ of the heart and the more subtle faculties of the heart. That said, the physical heart and subtle heart are not separate in my view—they are distinct manifestations of one unified Reality.

10. John of the Cross, *The Collected Works of St. John of the Cross*, trans. Kieran Kavanaugh and Otilio Rodriguez (Washington, DC: ICS Publications, 1991), 114.

11. Fyodor Dostoevsky, *The Brothers Karamazov: A Novel in Four Parts With Epilogue*, trans. Richard Pevear and Larissa Volokhonsky (New York: Farrar, Straus and Giroux, 2002), 319–320.

12. T. S. Eliot, *Four Quartets* (New York: Harcourt, Brace and Company, 1943), 39.

13. William Shakespeare, *Hamlet*, 5.2.159–160.

14. René Descartes, *Discourse on Method*, trans. Donald A. Cress, 3rd ed. (Indianapolis: Hackett Publishing, 1998), 19.

15. "Past Deans of the Faculty of Medicine," Harvard Medical School, accessed June 20, 2023, https://hms.harvard.edu/about-hms/office-dean/past-deans-faculty-medicine.

16. Venita Ramirez, Geoff Fitch, and Terri O'Fallon, "Causal Leadership: A Natural Emergence from Later Stages of Awareness" (paper presentation, the Integral Theory Conference, San Francisco, CA, May 15, 2013).

17. See Stephen W. Porges, *The Polyvagal Theory: Neurophysiological Foundations of Emotions, Attachment, Communication, and Self-Regulation* (New York: W. W.

Norton and Company, 2011).

18. Daniel P. Brown and David S. Elliott, *Attachment Disturbances in Adults: Treatment for Comprehensive Repair* (New York: W. W. Norton and Company, 2016), 289.

FIRST INTERLUDE

1. Joseph Smith to William W. Phelps, November 27, 1832, The Joseph Smith Papers, accessed May 9, 2023, https://www.josephsmithpapers.org/paper-summary/letter-to-william-w-phelps-27-november-1832/4.

CHAPTER 3

1. Gavin D. Flood, *An Introduction to Hinduism* (New York : Cambridge University Press, 1996), 94–95.

2. Michael Witzel, "Shamanism in Northern and Southern Eurasia: Their Distinctive Methods of Change of Consciousness," *Social Science Information* 50, no. 1 (2011): 43.

3. Cynthia Bourgeault, *The Wisdom Jesus: Transforming Heart and Mind—A New Perspective on Christ and His Message* (Boston: Shambhala, 2008), 25.

4. Thomas Keating, *Open Mind, Open Heart: The Contemplative Dimension of the Gospel* (New York: Continuum, 1995), 20.

5. Eugene England, "That They Might Not Suffer: The Gift of Atonement," Dialogue: *A Journal of Mormon Thought* 1, no. 3 (1966): 141–155.

6. David Rolph Seely, "William Tyndale and the Language of At-one-ment," in *The King James Bible and the Restoration*, ed. Kent P. Jackson (Provo, UT: Religious Studies Center, Brigham Young University, 2011), 25–42.

7. Keating, *Open Mind, Open Heart*, 21–26.

8. Philo Dibble, in "Recollections of the Prophet Joseph Smith," *Juvenile Instructor*, May 15, 1892, 303.

9. Dibble, in "Recollections," 304.

10. Frederick S. Perls, *Gestalt Therapy Verbatim*, ed. Joe Wysong (Highland, NY: Gestalt Journal, 1992), 37.

11. John Yates, Matthew Immergut, and Jeremy Graves, *The Mind Illuminated: A*

Complete Meditation Guide Integrating Buddhist Wisdom and Brain Science for Greater Mindfulness (New York: Simon and Schuster, 2017), 201–203.

12. The Living Bible (Wheaton, IL: Tyndale House Publishers, 2011).

13. Lao-Tzu, *Tao Te Ching*, trans. Stephen Mitchell (New York: HarperCollins, 1988), chap. 9.

CHAPTER 4

1. For a beautiful treatment of the topic of recognition, see Cynthia Bourgeault, *The Wisdom Jesus: Transforming Heart and Mind—a New Perspective on Christ and His Message* (Boston: Shambhala Publications, 2008), 1-12.

2. Mary Oliver, "Wild Geese," line 18.

3. Compare Kabir Edmund Helminski, *Living Presence: The Sufi Path to Mindfulness and the Essential Self*, rev. ed. (New York: A TarcherPerigee Book, 2017), 215. Helminski writes, "The heart is the individualized, manifesting part of the Universal Intelligence."

4. Lynn C. Bauman, *The Gospel of Thomas: Wisdom of the Twin*, 2nd ed., Logion 2 (Ashland, OR: White Cloud Press, 2012), 7.

5. Cynthia Bourgeault, *The Heart of Centering Prayer: Nondual Christianity in Theory and Practice* (Boulder: Shambhala, 2016), 62.

6. Herbert Marshall McLuhan, *Understanding Media: The Extensions of Man* (New York: New American Library, 1964), 23.

7. William Blake, *The Marriage of Heaven and Hell* (Boston: John W. Luce and Company, 1906), 14.

8. For an in-depth treatment of this topic, see David R. Shanks, *The Psychology of Associative Learning* (Cambridge: Cambridge University Press, 1995).

9. Helminski, *Living Presence*, 205.

10. William James, *The Varieties of Religious Experience: A Study in Human Nature* (New York: Modern library, 1902), 378–379.

11. Bourgeault, *Heart of Centering Prayer*, 84.

12. Lynn Bauman, *Keys to the Gospel Tradition: Metanoia* (online publication of the Oriental Orthodox Order in the West, rev. 2022), 7.

13. Thomas Merton, *Thoughts in Solitude*, 1st British ed. (London: Burns and Oates, 1958), 79.

14. "The Hidden Words: Bahá'u'lláh," trans. Shoghi Effendi, part 1, no. 59, accessed June 28, 2023, www.bahai.org/r/804011987.

15. Quoted by Adyashanti, *Falling into Grace : Insights on the End of Suffering* (Boulder, CO: Sounds True, Inc., 2011), 6–7.

CHAPTER 5

1. I highly recommend Bruce Tift's masterpiece, *Already Free: Buddhism Meets Psychotherapy on the Path to Liberation* (Boulder, CO: Sounds True, 2015), for a full treatment of this topic.

2. For an insightful treatment of this topic, see Thomas Keating, *Invitation to Love: The Way of Christian Contemplation* (New York: Continuum, 2000), 5–13.

3. Lao-Tzu, *Tao Te Ching*, trans. Stephen Mitchell (New York: HarperCollins, 1988), chap. 9.

4. Lynn Baumann (translator), *Keys to the Gospel Tradition: Metanoia* (online publication of the Oriental Orthodox Order in the West, rev. 2022), 1.

5. The Living Bible (Wheaton, IL: Tyndale House Publishers, 2011).

SECOND INTERLUDE

1. "O My Father," *Hymns*, no. 292.

2. "O My Father," *Hymns*, no. 292.

CHAPTER 6

1. Ken Wilber, *A Theory of Everything: An Integral Vision for Business, Politics, Science, and Spirituality*, Later prt. ed. (Boston: Shambhala, 2001).

2. Joseph B. Wirthlin, "Concern for the One," *Ensign or Liahona*, May 2008, https://www.churchofjesuschrist.org/study/general-conference/2008/04/concern-for-the-one?lang=eng.

3. I'm referring specifically to the work of Jean Piaget, Lawrence Kohlberg, and

Robert Kegan, respectively.

4. To my knowledge, Cook-Greuter does not use the language "zero-person perspective," but I find it to be a helpful concept. Among other things, it opens a space for spiritual teachings from the great Wisdom traditions, including the no self in Buddhism as well as *self-forgetting* in the context of Christian contemplation.

5. Thomas Metzinger, "Minimal Phenomenal Experience: Meditation, Tonic Alertness, and the Phenomenology of 'Pure' Consciousness," *Philosophy and the Mind Sciences* 1, no. 1 (2020): 7–8.

6. In the following sections, I will suggest practices to help the reader more fully embody the energies and qualities of each person perspective. I do not provide practices for zero-person perspective, however, because in my experience, initially accessing this aspect of our being requires sensitive and skilled guidance from a qualified teacher. The interested reader may consider attending certain intensive meditation retreats under expert guidance to familiarize themselves with this fascinating territory of human consciousness and development.

7. This formulation of human development is best articulated by John Kesler and his peerless Integral Polarity Practice. I owe so much of my current understanding to him and his body of work.

8. Margaret S. Mahler, Fred Pine, and Anni Bergman, *The Psychological Birth of The Human Infant Symbiosis and Individuation* (Basic Books, 2000), 52–54.

9. Research shows that by the end of the first year of life, babies begin to develop the capacity for symbolic thinking, which thereby allows them to form a representation of themselves as well as the self in relationship with others. This theory of mind continues to develop throughout the rest of one's lifespan. See Daniel P. Brown and David S. Elliott, *Attachment Disturbances: Treatment for Comprehensive Repair* (New York: W. W. Norton & Company, 2016), 72.

10. I'm indebted to Rachael Givens Johnson for this artful phrasing.

11. Susanne R. Cook-Greuter, "Nine Levels of Increasing Embrace in Ego Development: A Full-Spectrum Theory of Vertical Growth and Meaning Making" (unpublished manuscript, December 2013), PDF file, 18.

12. Joseph Campbell, *The Hero with a Thousand Faces* (Princeton, NJ: Princeton University Press, 1972), 391.

13. Brigham Young, in *Journal of Discourses*, 9:150.

14. Robert Kegan, *The Evolving Self: Problem and Process in Human Development* (Harvard University Press, 1982), 31.

15. Paul F. Knitter, *Without Buddha I Could Not Be a Christian* (Oxford: Oneworld, 2009), xiii.

16. Susanne R. Cook-Greuter, *Postautonomous Ego Development: A Study of Its Nature and Measurement* (Integral Publishers, 2010), 56.

17. Because the fifth- and sixth-person perspectives are statistically rare, I will not provide explicit practices for them in this short introduction to development. For the reader interested in exploring these aspects of our humanity, I highly recommend John Kesler's Integral Polarity Practice and Terri O'Fallon's Stages model.

18. I am deeply indebted to Dr. Terri O'Fallon and her pioneering efforts to work out the fine distinctions in this range of human development.

19. Lex Hixon, *Coming Home: The Experience of Enlightenment in Sacred Traditions* (Larson Publications, 1995), 101.

CHAPTER 7

1. Sri Aurobindo, *The Synthesis of Yoga* (Twin Lakes, WI: Lotus Press, 1992), 334.

2. Anna Freud and Cecil Baines, *The Ego and the Mechanisms of Defence* (New York: International Universities Press, 1946), 128.

3. Lex Hixon, *Coming Home: The Experience of Enlightenment in Sacred Traditions* (Burdett, NY: Larson Publications, 1995), 136.

4. Hixon, *Coming Home*, 136.

5. See William Blake, *The Marriage of Heaven and Hell* ([Coral Gables, Fla.], [University of Miami Press], 1963), 131.

6. Hixon, *Coming Home*, 137.

7. Joseph Smith, in *History of the Church*, 6:428.

8. Quoted in Olivier Clément, *The Roots of Christian Mysticism: Texts from the Patristic Era with Commentary*, 2nd ed. (Hyde Park, NY: New City Press, 2016), 273.

OTHER WORK BY THOMAS MCCONKIE

Navigating Mormon Faith Crisis (book)

Mindfulness+ with Thomas McConkie (podcast)

Transformations of Faith (online course)

For retreats and other offerings,
visit <u>lowerlightswisdom.org</u>.

About the Author

THOMAS WIRTHLIN MCCONKIE is an author, developmental researcher, and meditation teacher. As a teenager, he met his first teacher and has been practicing for over twenty-five years under masters in the traditions of Sufism, Buddhism and Christian contemplation, among others. Thomas is the founder of Lower Lights School of Wisdom, a nonprofit organization committed to sharing ancient and modern teachings from the world's Wisdom traditions. He is currently researching and writing on the topic of transformative spiritual practice at Harvard Divinity School. He lives with his wife, two kids, and rescue dog.